THE MOST PROMINENT DUTCHMAN IN EGYPT

Sidestone Press

THE MOST PROMINENT DUTCHMAN IN EGYPT

Jan Herman Insinger and the Egyptian collection in Leiden

Maarten J. Raven

PAPERS ON ARCHAEOLOGY OF THE
LEIDEN MUSEUM OF ANTIQUITIES

© 2018 Maarten J. Raven, Rijksmuseum van Oudheden

PALMA: Papers on Archaeology of the Leiden Museum of Antiquities (volume 19)

Published by Sidestone Press, Leiden
www.sidestone.com

Imprint: Sidestone Press

Lay-out & cover design: Sidestone Press

Photography: Peter Jan Bomhof, Anneke J. de Kemp and Robbert-Jan Looman

Photographs cover:
Portrait of Jan Herman Insinger at the age of fifty (Studio C. Ruf, R. Ganz Nachfolger, Zurich, 31 August 1904, from a reproduction in the Archives of the RMO) and coffin for a falcon mummy, Graeco-Roman period, h. 48, w. 29, l. 55 cm (inv.no. F 1929/12.32).

ISBN 978-90-8890-551-3 (softcover)
ISBN 978-90-8890-552-0 (hardcover)
ISBN 978-90-8890-553-7 (PDF e-book)

ISSN 2034-550X

Contents

Contents

Introduction 7

Chapter I:
Concise biography of Jan Herman Insinger 11
    1. Banker's son (1856-1879) 11
    2. Nile traveller (1879-1883) 11
    3. True friend (1883-1888) 15
    4. Land-owner in Luxor (1888-1903) 18
    5. Grumpy old man (1903-1918) 20

Chapter II:
Jan Herman Insinger as a purveyor of antiquities for the RMO 23
    1. Exploits with Schelling (1882) 23
    2. Manuscripts and mummies (1886) 26
    3. Ostraca and textiles (1888) 32
    4. Purchase of a papyrus (1895) 34
    5. Potsherds and prehistory (1897-1901) 37
    6. Donations by descendants (1929-1957) 43

Chapter III:
Jan Herman Insinger and the antiquities trade of his time 49
    1. Dealer or donator? 49
    2. Abiding by the law 50
    3. Missed opportunities 54
    4. Conclusions 56

Appendix I: List of acquisitions from Insinger 59

Appendix II: Translations of letters written by Insinger 61

Abbreviations 85

Bibliography 87

Indices 91

RMO inv.no. F 1929/12.1: granodiorite statue of Osiris, Late period, h. 36.5 cm.

Introduction

The National Museum of Antiquities of the Netherlands (*Rijksmuseum van Oudheden*, henceforth abbreviated as RMO) in Leiden was founded in 1818.[1] The decision to establish a Dutch national collection of antiquities was made by King William I, the first monarch of the Netherlands after the Napoleonic period, during which the country was occupied by the French. By 1840, the pioneer years of the museum, when this institution defined its own position in the Dutch cultural constellation and established its international reputation as one of the foremost archaeological museums in the world, had definitely come to an end. Caspar Reuvens, the founding father of the museum and its first director, died unexpectedly in 1835, leaving the administration to his able assistant Conrad Leemans. The latter, however, was not appointed as the official successor until 1839. Twenty years after its foundation, the museum finally acquired a proper building for the display of its treasures in Breestraat 18, which opened its doors to the public on 7 August 1838. Two years later, on 7 October 1840, King William I, who had been the chief maecenas of the newly-founded museum during its formative years, abdicated. As a result of these three events, the RMO definitely entered a new era.

Although the collections continued to grow, the pace was markedly slower than during the preceding two decennia. This was mainly due to the changing economic situation in the Netherlands, which had lost its southern provinces as a result of the Belgian insurrection of 1830. Moreover, the new sovereign, William II, had a quite different personality than his father and did not personally support the museum's ambitions in the field of acquisition – as the latter had repeatedly done. Instead, he left the matter to endless negotiations between the museum's administration and the Ministry. And finally, Conrad Leemans likewise had a far less impetuous temperament than his predecessor Reuvens, concentrating on consolidation of the *status quo* and on publication of the collections rather than on audacious purchases, excavations, and similar adventures. Because he continued the office of director until 1891, he can be said to have dominated the greater part of the nineteenth century history of the RMO. Moreover, he left an equal mark on the National Museum of Ethnology (likewise housed in Leiden), where he served as director from 1859 to 1880. In the RMO, he was succeeded by his curator, Willem Pleyte, who ushered the museum into the new century until his death in 1903.

All three 19th-century directors of the RMO excelled as scholars with a broad archaeological expertise (Fig. 0.1). Each of them also had a special relationship with the emerging discipline of Egyptology, and certainly the two latter ones devoted the better part of their academic work to that field of study.[2] Still, neither of them personally visited the antiquities along the Nile. It may be said that Reuvens lacked the time, Leemans the spirit, and Pleyte the health to visit Egypt in person. Had Reuvens survived longer, he would undoubtedly have undertaken such a voyage. In the case of the long-lived Leemans age was clearly not an issue, but he seems to have satisfied himself with the

---

1 For the following, see Halbertsma 2003, 141-152; ter Keurs/Wirtz 2018.
2 All three are unreservedly regarded as Egyptologists by Bierbrier 2012: see the entries on pages 461-462, 317, and 437-438, respectively.

Fig. 0.1. The three directors of the RMO during the 19th century: from left to right Caspar Reuvens, Conrad Leemans, and Willem Pleyte.

existence of an armchair archaeologist instead. Pleyte, on the other hand, was requested by Leemans to start his museum career mainly in the Dutch department. When eventually Leemans was pensioned and Pleyte was more at liberty to travel abroad, he certainly intended to leave for a Nile trip,[3] but his good health was already gone and his plans never materialized.

Under the circumstances, it is remarkable that the Leiden Museum managed to bring together one of the best Egyptian collections in the world. Clearly, this was largely the achievement of a number of very capable middlemen with a good knowledge of the art market, a talent for negotiating, and access to the social circles where the commerce in antiquities took place. The first person answering this description was Jean Emile Humbert (1771-1839), who never visited Egypt but counts as one of the discoverers of Carthage and later snapped up the museum's acquisitions in Italy.[4] The second was Jan Herman Insinger (1854-1918), who lived in Egypt for almost forty years and became the RMO's eyes and ears in the country of the Pharaohs.

Jan Herman Insinger was a well-known character in the history of Egyptology, mainly because his name has been linked forever with a famous demotic wisdom papyrus now in Leiden.[5] Otherwise he was a rather inconspicuous figure: though he is mentioned by many of his contemporaries, biographical notes on Insinger rarely surpass a few lines[6] and can be quite inaccurate. However, a lot of information can be gathered from the Archives of the RMO and of the National Museum of Ethnology, both in Leiden, and from the former archive of the Aardrijkskundig Genootschap (Geographical Society), now in the Amsterdam University Library. The latter Society also printed one of Insinger's travel accounts,[7] and there are various other sources, both published and unpublished ones. These documents enabled the present author to sketch a brief biography of this fascinating figure in 1991, in the framework of an article focusing on Insinger's activities as a photographer.[8] A much fuller biography could be given in the 2004 re-edition of the said travel account.[9] Unfortunately, the latter is in Dutch and lacks references to the original source material, whereas the former appeared in a journal which is hard to get in most libraries. Therefore, the context of the present volume seems to present a good

---

3 As transpires from his correspondence with Insinger; see RMO Archives, dispatched letters, 1896/169, 1898/98.
4 See Halbertsma 1995; Halbertsma 2003, 71-111.
5 See below, 34-37.
6 *Cf.* Bierbrier 2012, 273; Carstens 2014, 349-350. See now Thompson 2015, 124-125.
7 Insinger 1885.
8 Raven 1991, especially 16-19.
9 Insinger 2004, especially 1-15.

opportunity to sum up the evidence once again in a more scholarly fashion and in a language which can be understood by a larger audience. Moreover, it has been possible to update the former versions in several respects.

New is the focus placed in the present volume on Insinger's activities as an art collector. Though he has often been characterised as an outright art dealer,[10] we shall see that there is no evidence that these activities had a marked commercial flavour. Instead, Insinger can be regarded as a maecenas of the Leiden Museum, whereas no objects formerly from his collections have come to light in other museums. Thus, a study of this aspect of his manifold interests is mainly relevant for the information it provides on the growth of the Egyptian treasures in Leiden. It is very satisfying, therefore, that the present study could be published in the PALMA series devoted to the collections and research projects of the RMO, and I want to thank the editors of the series for providing me with this opportunity.

---

10   Wilson 1964, 102, 223; James 1992, 76; Bierbrier 2012, 273.

Chapter I

Concise biography of Jan Herman Insinger

1. Banker's son (1856-1879)

Jan Herman Insinger was born in Amsterdam on 12 May 1854 (Fig. I.1).[1] He was a descendant of a well-to-do family, originally from Bückeburg in Germany, where his ancestors can be traced as early as the 17th century. In 1801 Jan Herman's great-grandfather Hermann Albrecht founded the Insinger & Co. merchant and banking firm in Amsterdam, which still exists nowadays. His grandson (also called Herman Albrecht and Jan Herman's father) was best known as director of the Amsterdam Canal Company, which would dig the North Sea Canal linking the Dutch capital with the sluices at IJmuiden, opened in 1876. He was also active as a politician in the city-council of Amsterdam, the county council of the province of Noord-Holland, and the Lower House of parliament. In 1860 he purchased the estate of Pijnenburg near Baarn, a country-seat of 17th century origin which was used as a summer house by the Insinger family.

Jan Herman was the eldest of seven children: six boys and a girl. Although they grew up in great affluence, several of the children had the bad luck to be infected with tuberculosis, allegedly as a result of drinking contaminated milk. This caused the early death of three of Jan Herman's brothers, between 1878 and 1881, whereas his own health was also seriously affected by the disease. Therefore his parents decided to save at least their first-born son by sending him to the beneficial climate of Egypt, which attracted so many consumptives at the time. Fortunately, this change of air proved to be effective in his case, too, and Insinger would live to the age of sixty-four, dying in Cairo on 27 October 1918. It was not just his health which profited from his parents' wise decision, though: Egyptology owes much to Insinger's prolonged stay along the Nile, because the young man was soon captivated by the country's antiquities and sought to make himself useful to archaeology. In the course of forty years he witnessed numerous unique events in the capacity of a traveller, photographer, art collector, and intimate friend of several illustrious scholars.

2. Nile traveller (1879-1883)

Insinger first arrived in Egypt in 1879,[2] in a period of rising tensions between the Egyptian government and the European powers. The country went through a political and financial crisis, which had been caused by the over-ambitious infrastructural projects

---

1 For the following, see *Nederland's Patriciaat* 72 (1988), 249-279, especially 273.
2 This date, inferred from other evidence in my previous studies (Raven 1991, 16 with n. 32; Insinger 2004, 2), can now be confirmed on the basis of a passing reference by Insinger himself in one of his columns written for the newspaper *Het Nieuws van den Dag* (14 November 1887, page 2), from which we may conclude that he was definitely in the country by the beginning of December 1879.

of the prodigal Khedive (Viceroy) Ismail,³ notably the digging of the Suez Canal which was inaugurated in 1869, the construction of the first railways, and the realization of fashionable 'Belle Époque' extensions in Alexandria, Cairo, and the canal city of Ismailiya. Military adventures in the Sudan and Ethiopia led to further debts, and at the request of Britain and France the extravagant Ismail was deposed by the Turkish Sultan in June 1879. He was succeeded by his ineffective son Tewfik,⁴ who was then forced to reform the country by the European dual powers, which only sought to protect their own interests. Inevitably, this led to dissatisfaction among the Egyptian population and the military, and to a distinct anti-foreign movement. Tensions also spread between the French, who had played an important part in Egyptian politics ever since the Napoleonic expedition and who traditionally led the Antiquities Service, and the English, who gradually transformed the Nilotic region in order to create a British protectorate. In spite of these disorders, the country still attracted extensive numbers of tourists, whereas cities like Alexandria and Cairo housed large foreign communities.

Even though Insinger's self-imposed exile cannot always have been easy, his financial means and social background helped him to make the best of it. Thus he was immediately received into the better circles of the European community in Cairo. Upon his arrival he still looked like a dying man, but his health was soon restored and he started to enjoy his new environment. Unfortunately, even in Cairo winters were too damp and cold for a consumptive, so that he decided to hire a boat and explore Upper Egypt with its hotter and drier climate. This nomadic way of life enabled Insinger to acquire a better knowledge of the country than most of his contemporaries. Summers were usually spent in Cairo, Alexandria, or the Nile Delta, and his improved health even allowed incidental visits to Italy or his relatives in Holland.

Right from the beginning, Insinger took a great interest in the Egyptian antiquities. This is demonstrated by the extent of his travels, which brought him to places hardly ever visited by other Europeans.⁵ He also established a close relationship with the successive directors of the Cairo Museum (at the time housed at Bulaq, Cairo's harbour suburb) and the Antiquities Service, both of which had been founded by the Frenchman Auguste Mariette in 1858-1859.⁶ After his death on 18 January 1881, Mariette was succeeded by his compatriot Gaston Maspero (1846-1916),⁷ and it is this second director who

Fig. I.1. Portrait of Jan Herman Insinger at the age of fifty (Studio C. Ruf, R. Ganz Nachfolger, Zurich, 31 August 1904). From a reproduction in the Archives of the RMO.

informs us about the first exploits of Jan Herman Insinger, quoting from a letter written at his request by the latter, twenty years after the event.⁸ Here the Dutchman records his memories of his first trip upstream in the months of January to April, 1880, probably on board of a hired *dahabiya*⁹ shared with other travellers. After passing the full length of Upper Egypt and crossing the first cataract at Aswan, this voyage brought him to the next rapids at Wadi Halfa, which mark the border between Lower Nubia with its numerous pharaonic remains and the rarely visited region of Upper Nubia. So far, this was already becoming a standard tour at the time, and Insinger could use the recently published account by the British novelist Amelia Edwards as a guidebook.¹⁰ He also kept his own

---

3   *Cf.* Carstens 2014, 357-358.
4   *Ibid.* 657-658.
5   As can be seen from the list of places where he was active as a photographer: see Raven 1991, 21-22. *Cf.* also Raven 2009.
6   Bierbrier 2012, 355-357.
7   Bierbrier 2012, 359-361; Thompson 2015, 4-6.

8   Maspero 1901, 148-152.
9   A long ship with lateen sails and a large cabin, used by tourists as semi-permanent lodging or for travelling along the Nile.
10 Insinger used the Tauchnitz edition (Edwards 1878), as stated in Maspero 1901, 149.

Fig. I.2. Great temple of Abu Simbel. Photo by J.H. Insinger, 12.3 x 17.3 cm, Archives RMO.

detailed notes, but unfortunately lost track of them later,[11] and they have apparently not survived.[12]

In December 1880 Insinger again set sail to Nubia in the company of four other tourists, among whom was the French photographer Daniel Héron.[13] Insinger had also brought his own photographic equipment, and pictures taken by both travel companions later provided illustrations for a number of books.[14] Again the expedition went as far as the temples of Abu Simbel in the Wadi Halfa area (Fig. I.2.), and from there gradually returned northwards. While in Nubia, the travellers were told at several places about the existence of a legendary temple said to be located at half a day's journey west of the Nile, a rumour also recorded by Amelia Edwards. After dropping their travel companions in Cairo in February 1881, Héron and Insinger therefore provided themselves with a proper excavation permit (doubtless from the office of the Antiquities Service, in which case it may have been one of the first documents signed by the new director Maspero) and with a letter of recommendation from the Dutch consul Anslijn.[15] They

---

11 Maspero 1901, 148.
12 Oral communication by the Insinger family. The 1883 printed account (now Insinger 2004) is a notable exception.
13 *Cf.* Perez 1988, 177, who states that Héron worked together with Insinger (178).
14 Photos taken by Héron during this trip were used to illustrate books by Maspero (Maspero 1895, 123, 181; Maspero 1897, 296-297, 351, 410-412, 530, 555) and by the French traveller Elisée Reclus. Maspero also used a number of Insinger's photos dated 1881 (as well as numerous later ones; see Maspero 1895, 14-15, 28, 481; Maspero 1897, 409, 411-412, 415, 519, 525, 530, 699), while some others may be wrongly dated because they depict sites lying to the south of Wadi Halfa (Maspero 1897, 231, 377).
15 Algemeen Rijksarchief (National Archives), The Hague, Correspondence with the diplomatic office in Egypt and the general consulate at Alexandria, 1861-1884, 2.05.30/13: letter of 20 February 1881.

then travelled back by train to Assiut, and from there by mail-boat to Aswan, where they picked up a local guide. However, the latter failed to identify the way, and after a short exploration on camelback around Maharaqqa the expedition was called off because of the increasing heat, whereupon the company returned to Cairo.

In the course of that same year Insinger married Mariam Mansour Hanna Daraoun.[16] She had been born in Lebanon in 1865, but nothing else is known about her. Political events must have overshadowed the marriage festivities.[17] In September the Khedive was besieged in his own palace and forced to call elections. Probably this explains why Insinger decided to take his wife with him on his next trip to Nubia; the third member of the party was a Dutch engineer working for the Alexandria Water Company, Antonie Johannes Schelling (1854-1883). This time the journey led him to Semna in the area of the Second Cataract, and again he met with a Nubian who pretended to know the way to the mysterious temple, adding that one had to leave the Nile at Aswan instead of further south. A last attempt was made to explore the monument in question, but after a 60 kilometre ride on camelback the party merely reached the small uninhabited oasis of Kurkur without spotting any ancient constructions. Thus, they returned to Cairo in the spring of 1882 with nothing achieved, though the local population had been so much impressed by the exploits of Abu Shanab (Father of the Moustache = Insinger) that they were still talking about it fifteen years later.[18]

Even so, this futile exploration had some positive results. Both Insinger and his travel companion Schelling had picked up or purchased some antiquities *en route*. They showed their finds to Maspero in Cairo, who then gave them permission to export these few objects. Insinger spent part of summer in Italy that year. From there he wrote to Pleyte in the Leiden Museum, announcing that he would send these antiquities as a present, together with the first batch of prints of his photographs.[19] The letter represents the first known contact between the collectionneur and the museum, and accordingly its tone is still rather formal. This occasion marks the beginning of a long series of letters and a great number of consignments of antiquities for the Leiden Museum, which will be discussed in the next chapter. Nine days earlier, Schelling had already written to Lindor Serrurier, then director of the Leiden Museum of Ethnography, announcing a similar dispatch of objects for that institution (although it included some samples of pottery for the Museum of Antiquities, too).[20] This letter proves that Serrurier officially authorized Schelling to make purchases on behalf of the museum; it is unclear whether Insinger was carrying a similar permit signed by Leemans.

Insinger's stay in Italy had probably much to do with the political situation in Egypt that summer.[21] Britain and France used the rise to power of the new Egyptian government, which was dominated by the distinctly anti-western Defense Secretary Urabi Pasha, as a pretext to gather a fleet in front of Alexandria harbour. In June, when some Europeans were killed during riots, all 15.000 westerners were advised to leave the country as soon as possible. One month later, on July 11-12, Alexandria was bombarded, and peace was not restored until September, when Urabi's camp in the Nile Delta was stormed by British troops. Egypt now became a British protectorate, and the Europeans gradually returned. Among them were Insinger and Schelling. The former again undertook a journey southwards at the end of the year.

It is unknown whether on that occasion he was accompanied by his wife. What we do know is that at the beginning of 1883 he wrote from Wadi Halfa to Schelling,[22] who had assumed a new position in Cairo in the department of public works of that city and therefore was unable to join the party. The letter specified that Insinger had stomach complaints and was awaiting the next tourist steamer of Cook's, which always had a doctor on board. Schelling expected that the combination with his lung problems would be enough to force him to return northwards. But on the contrary, Insinger left his *dahabiya* on February 8 for an intrepid tour through Upper Nubia: first on camelback to el-Urdi (New Dongola), and from there on a ramshackle cargo boat to el-Debba, not returning in Wadi Halfa until March 24. This is the only travel for which a diary has been preserved, because two years later Insinger's notes were published in the journal of the

---

16 Insinger himself, quoted in Maspero 1901, 150, speaks of 'my wife' when referring to the winter of 1881-1882. However, *Nederland's Patriciaat* 72 (1988), 273 mentions a marriage date of 5 July 1892 in Cairo, which postdates the birth of the three daughters Frederika Mina Hanna (1884), Frederika Johanna (1885), and Olga Charlotte Hanna (1887). Possibly the marriage was only properly registered a few months before the birth of a son, Edmond Herman Deodatus, later in 1892.
17 These troubles are known as the Urabi revolt; see Carstens 2014, 681-682.
18 Maspero 1901, 147.
19 See Appendix II, letter no. **1**. For the Insinger photographs now in the RMO Archives, see Raven 1991.

20 National Museum of Ethnology, Leiden, Archives, letter of Schelling to Serrurier, 1 June 1882. I wish to thank Graciella Roosien for sending me a copy of the letter, and Annette Schmidt for permission to quote from it.
21 See n. 17 above. *Cf.* Thompson 2015, 2-4.
22 This is mentioned in a letter to Serrurier written by Schelling on 14 February 1883, now kept in the archives of the National Museum of Ethnology, Leiden.

Dutch Geographical Society.²³ Under the circumstances, it was a remarkable act of bravery, not only because of Insinger's poor health but also because he decided to travel through these rarely visited stretches of the Nile valley alone with a small team of locals: several camel-drivers, a guide, an interpreter, a servant, and a cook. Moreover, the whole of the Sudan was in a state of revolt since in 1881 Mohammed Ahmed ibn Abdallah from Dongola had announced he was the long-expected Mahdi (redeemer) who would help the country to shake off the Turkish-British occupation.²⁴ When Insinger left, the British were already drawing together their troops for a counter-attack, which could not prevent that by the end of the same year the western provinces of Kordofan and Darfur fell into the hands of the Mahdist insurgents. Perhaps Insinger realized this would be his final chance to see the antiquities of the Nubian districts of Sukkot, Mahas, and Dongola, not only because of the prospect of war but also in view of his own health and his family situation.

3. True friend (1883-1888)

That summer, there was an outbreak of cholera in Egypt, so that Insinger decided to spend some time in self-imposed quarantine, moored near Damietta in the Nile Delta.²⁵ He now owned his own boat, a *dahabiya* called *De Meermin* (The Mermaid), which had probably been purchased because of the expected extension of his family (Fig. I.3).²⁶ In spite of the threatening situation in the Sudan, he again visited Nubia the succeeding winter, apparently travelling upstream as far as Wadi Halfa again. Upon his way back, Insinger met a man who would become a new travelling companion, *viz.* the American

Fig. I.3. Dahabiya de Meermin. Photo by J.H. Insinger, 11.8 x 16.4 cm, Archives RMO.

Charles Edwin Wilbour (1833-1896).²⁷ After having made a fortune in business, Wilbour spent the last twenty years of his life in Egypt and France. He became a pupil of the Egyptologist Maspero, whom he regularly accompanied on the steamer of the Antiquities Service. Later he owned his own steamship, and it was therefore inevitable that he would meet with the Insinger family sooner or later. Wilbour's letters, which were edited by Jean Capart, give the impression that they actually met in Assiut on March 30, 1884,²⁸ and visited the monuments of Saqqara together one month later.

Upon Insinger's return in Cairo, his daughter Frederika Mina Hanna was born. She was probably called after her father's younger brother Frederik, who obtained a post as apprentice interpreter at the consulate in Cairo that same year and therefore may have been present.²⁹ Another relative who would soon come to live with the family was Insinger's sister-in-law Yasmeen. That, and the birth of the other daughters in the years 1885 and 1887 soon made the boat too small already. It is unknown whether the young family travelled upstream again by the end of that year, but such a Nile cruise is certainly recorded for the winter of 1885-1886, thanks to letters written to the RMO from el-Balyana in December, from Aswan in January, and from Assiut in March.³⁰

---

23 Insinger 1885, re-edited by the present author as Insinger 2004 on the basis of an offprint kindly supplied by the Insinger family. At the time, it was supposed this was a privately printed edition for circulation within the family (Insinger 2004, viii). However, this can now be refuted because of the identification of the original place of publication by Saskia Asser (Huis Marseille, Museum for Photography, Amsterdam) in 2016.
24 *Cf.* Carstens 2014, 436-438.
25 According to Wilbour, in: Capart 1936, 310.
26 *Loc.cit.*: 'Mr Insinger spent all last summer on his dahabeeyeh, staying at Damietta during the cholera. He has now spent most of his time on the Nile for five years, and is as black as an Arab.' *Cf.* Archives RMO 22.3/2, Insinger photos, nos. 34a-c; reproduced in Insinger 2004, fig. 12. The ship was called after the family coat-of-arms which shows a merman (*Nederland's Patriciaat* 72 (1988), 249). According to Wilbour in a letter written at the beginning of 1886 (Capart 1936, 352) the ship was then two years old ('Insinger, the Dutchman of years past, who instead of dying, as we thought he must, is having a good time in his dahabeeyeh, which, only two years old, is already growing too small for his increasing family'). There are also photographs of a *dahabiya* called Eva (Archives RMO 22.3/6, Insinger photos, nos. 31-32, 34), which may be a hired vessel of Insinger's early years in Egypt.

27 Bierbrier 2012, 576-577; Thompson 2015, 58-60.
28 Capart 1936, 301: 'The Dutchman, Mr Insinger, came to see us'. Yet on page 310, Capart wrongly asserts the first meeting was on April 12, the date when the two men visited Saqqara together with Sophie Mariette. Wilbour's first visit to Egypt was in 1880 (Wilson 1964, 102), and it is hard to believe the two men did not meet before.
29 Wilbour calls this brother 'Fritz' (Capart 1936, 432, 467, 482), and I admit I added to the confusion by assuming this was his nickname for Jan Herman (Insinger 2004, 10), which is improbable.
30 Appendix II, letters nos. **4-6**.

Fig. I.4. *Group portrait of (from left to right) De Rochemonteix, Gayet, Insinger, Wilbour, and Maspero. Photo by Toda y Güell, made in Karnak 1886. Reproduced after Capart 1936.*

At the end of January, Insinger joined the inspection tour by Maspero, Wilbour, Grébaut and Bouriant, who had by then arrived in Luxor on board the steamer *Boulaq* (Fig. I.4).[31] Another person joining the company was the Catalan traveller Eduardo Toda y Güell,[32] who assisted in the clearing of the famous tomb of Sennedjem at Deir el-Medina in the first days of February.[33] Toda was asked to draw up an inventory of the finds, whereas Insinger took care of the photography of the newly-found tomb and of some of the objects.[34] We also know that in February Insinger undertook some photography for Wilbour in Luxor, el-Kab and Tod, Wilbour's steamer towing the *dahabiya*. The two friends visited Aswan, the Luxor temple, Abydos, and Akhmim together, where by mid-March Wilbour 'left him and his Syrienne and their two babies and her younger sister', adding that Insinger liked the hot weather and would not come northwards before May.[35]

A couple of weeks after Insinger's return to the capital, he got involved in a fascinating research project at the Cairo Museum. In 1881, Maspero had asked his assistant Emil Brugsch[36] to investigate the source of a steady stream of objects with royal names offered for sale in Luxor. The trail led to a family of notorious tomb-robbers by the name of Abd-er-Rasul, and after being heard by the police one of them was willing to disclose the

---

31 For Grébaut and Bouriant, see Bierbrier 2012, 223 and 75, respectively. Eugène Grébaut (1846-1915) was Director of the Institut Français d'Archéologie Orientale in Cairo at the time. Urbain Bouriant (1849-1903) started his career as assistant curator at the Bulaq Museum and became Grébaut's successor from 1886 to 1898.
32 Bierbrier 2012, 542.
33 Toda 1920 (Insinger mentioned on pages 146, 148); Esteva 2016, 120-151 (Insinger mentioned on page 122); *cf.* Mahmoud 2011 (Insinger mentioned on page 2).
34 Esteva 2016 erroneously attributes these photographs to Toda (pp. 120, 128 upper and lower, 130, 131 and 136 upper and lower can all by identified as originals by Insinger; see archives RMO 22.3/3 nos. 14b, 14c, 14e, 14h, 14l and 14k, respectively). *Cf.* the portrait of Toda on page 127 of the same book, and the group portraits on page 93. *Op.cit.* 25 quotes Toda's journal, where he refers to the good luck that he was able to use Insingers's photographic services. Other photographs by Insinger in Toda's archive are reproduced by Esteva 2016 on pp. 71, 85, 113, 167, 169, 171, 175-176, 178-184, 186-187, 198-201, 207, 212, 215, 220-221, 239-242, 244-251.
35 Capart 1936, 358-384 (quotation on page 379).
36 Bierbrier 2012, 83-84.

location of a hitherto unknown rock-tomb in the valley of Deir el-Bahari on Luxor's west bank. It proved to be a hiding-place of grave goods and mummies of about forty New Kingdom pharaohs and their relatives.[37] Such was the importance of this find that Brugsch decided to empty the underground galleries in no more than two days and to transport the whole contents instantly to the Museum at Bulaq, which had to be extended in order to house the new acquisitions. There most of them were kept for five years, though two of the mummies were already opened more or less clandestinely by Brugsch, who could not resist his curiosity and made use of Maspero's temporary absence; another mummy had to be unwrapped because it started decomposing.[38] These incidents convinced Maspero of the necessity to organize a series of dissections of the bodies in the summer of 1886. The first *séance* on June 1st was attended by the Egyptian Vice-Roy and by a whole number of high dignitaries, various ambassadors, etc. For a start, the mummy of Ramesses II was opened, an operation which took no more than a quarter of an hour as Maspero notes down with great satisfaction.[39]

Apparently, Insinger was not one of those present on that occasion, but he was invited to attend at least some of the other sessions on June 6, 9, 17, 19 and 20, when he made himself useful by taking measurements.[40] He owed the invitation to his personal friendship with Maspero and Brugsch. In fact the latter had already contacted him about the spectacular find in 1884: Brugsch was not only cheating his superior by opening mummies behind his back, he had also developed the habit of secretly taking clippings of the mummy wrappings and was now offering these for sale. Insinger contacted Pleyte about this, but the matter was considered to be too sensitive (Brugsch's name was not to be mentioned, and clearly Maspero knew nothing about it) and therefore the sale was not made.[41] However, the official dissections offered a fresh opportunity for taking samples of linen, and now in an aboveboard manner since the wrappings were not kept and all present were apparently allowed to help themselves to them before they were thrown away. Accordingly, Insinger could write to Leemans on July 15 that he planned to send

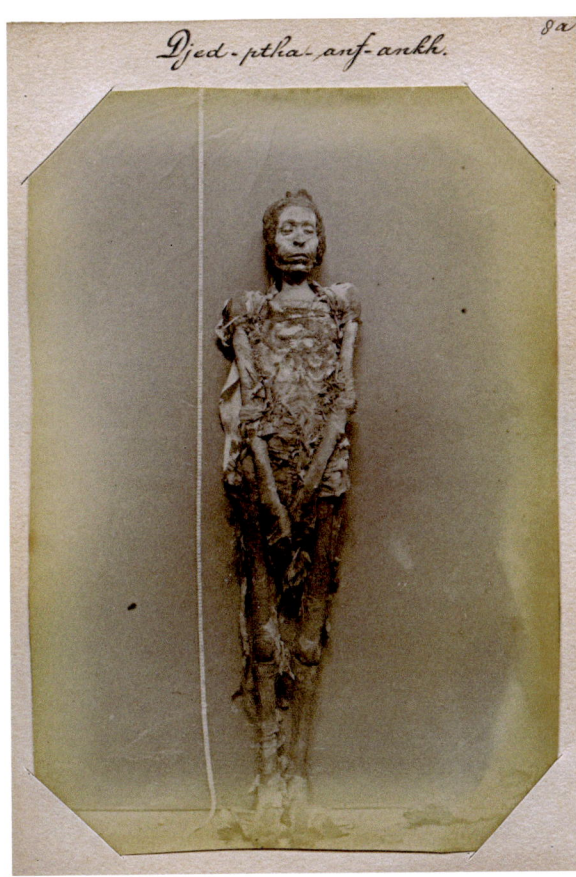

Fig. I.5. Mummy of Djedptahefankh during examination. Photo by J.H. Insinger, 17.1 x 12.3 cm, Archives RMO.

over various samples of textile, among which several taken from the mummies of Deir el-Bahari.[42] He also added that he would send copies of his anatomical measurements (these can no longer be found in the RMO Archives) and prints of the photographs which he took during the unwrappings. The official photographer recording the dissections was Emil Brugsch, and his prints indeed figure in the catalogue volume eventually published on the royal mummies by the Cairo Museum.[43] It is still not generally known that there exists a second set of photographs made by Insinger during those *séances* where he was present (Fig. I.5). These are now in the RMO Archives, having been sent in several instalments in 1888.[44]

The late summer of 1886 was marked by a visit to Rosetta and Alexandria.[45] Wilbour reports that Insinger

---

37 For the history of discovery of the so-called royal cachette, see Maspero 1889b, 511-523; *cf.* Thompson 2015, 8-10.
38 Maspero 1889b, 525.
39 *Ibid*. 525; see also footnote 2 which refers to the published *procès-verbal* giving a list of the invited guests.
40 *Ibid*. 528, 531, 541, 543, 561, 565, 574. A brief notice on the dissections written by Insinger himself appeared in *Het Nieuws van den Dag* of 3 August 1886; here he mentions that he spent almost every morning at the Bulaq Museum in this period.
41 Appendix II, letter no. **3**. For the notorious reputation of Brugsch, who was selling more antiquities from the museum and was also involved in the forgery of sculptures by the museum's restorers, see Fiechter 2005, 48-52.

42 Appendix II, letter no. **8**.
43 Smith 1912, with remark on page v.
44 Archives RMO, 22.3/3-6, with what was probably an earlier album registered as 22.3/2; see Raven 1991, 19-21.
45 *Het Nieuws van den Dag*, 3 August and 11 October 1886 (columns written on 11 July and 1 September, respectively).

was in Cairo upon his arrival there in November.[46] 'Insinger is a true friend', who invited Wilbour for dinner on board his *dahabiya* and showed him the photographs of the royal mummies. He also possessed a small steamboat now and helped to prepare Wilbour's own house-boat. After showing his father (who was over from Holland) and brother around in Saqqara, Insinger left upstream by the end of December, reaching Aswan by mid-February,[47] assisting Wilbour where he could, and helping him with his departure in April 1887. Apparently Wilbour paid him for his services, which included taking his *dahabiya* in tow with the steamer for part of the time.[48] The Insinger family resided in Cairo most of that summer.[49]

Wilbour was back by November 1887 and again the two friends left together for Upper Egypt, each with his own *puffpuff* (steamer) and *dahabiya*.[50] In the course of that winter they kept close contact, and Insinger helped Wilbour with repairs of his boat and by procuring him a new captain (a cousin of his own *ra'is*). His health was so bad that when they arrived at Beni Suef, he was unable to walk to town. Later he had to stay behind in Assiut (the terminal of the railway line), waiting for medicine sent from Cairo by his Dutch doctor, and he was in trouble for most of that winter. Even as late as the beginning of April, Wilbour remarked: 'Insinger's health was poor; I think that he suffered more than I have ever seen him before'.[51] He did not arrive in Luxor until the end of January 1888, and later visited Aswan for a while. That winter, Insinger spent considerably more of his time in Luxor because of some new developments: after almost ten years of living on the Nile, he had decided to build himself a house in Luxor, and he was 'hoping to finish three rooms so that he could sleep in it cold nights next winter'.[52] When they returned in Cairo by the end of April, Insinger's family was suffering from ophthalmia, and they were still in the capital in June and July.[53] Late summer or early autumn brought an excursion to Alexandria, where the boat was moored in the Mahmudieh canal, but Insinger fell ill and had to be taken to the local hospital with malaria.[54]

4. Land-owner in Luxor (1888-1903)

The winter of 1888-1889 was the last one spent in the usual way in the company of Wilbour, who met Insinger on the Nile close to Minia on November 20.[55] Insinger's health had recovered over summer ('He seems as well as last year'), and when the two companions visited Amarna together he made photographs the whole day inside one of the rock-tombs. They arrived in Luxor in December, where Insinger immediately resumed supervising the construction of his house. On January 12, Wilbour reported that the construction of the ground floor had already been finished, and two days later he visited the building site.[56] This project apparently took all Insinger's energy and he seems to have stayed behind. Wilbour himself travelled on, meeting his friend again ('he looks blacker and thinner than ever') at the end of May in Cairo, where Insinger was buying furniture for the house.[57] Accordingly, upon Wilbour's return the next winter, he could visit the Insingers properly installed in their new mansion, though it was still being extended and did not protect its inhabitants against the cold.[58]

It has long been unknown where exactly this house was situated and what it looked like. Recently, some new information has become available, partly because of some photographs sent over by Insinger's Canadian descendants (Fig. I.6),[59] partly as a result of additional research by dr Rob Demarée.[60] Its location has now been established as due south of the present-day Iberotel, where Insinger was able to buy a virgin plot along the Nile.[61] The house figures on several photographs and even films made by tourists at the time. After Insinger's death it became the summerhouse of the second wife of Sultan Hussein Kamel,[62] and was named Sultana Melek Palace after her. This lasted until the Egyptian revolution of 1952, when the house became a girls' school, and eventually a storehouse for water-melons. Some parts survived until the 1960s, when it was demolished. A vivid description in its glory days was published by G. van Stolk in the magazine *Neerlandia* of January 1904.[63] He states that Insinger was his own architect and built the house in several stages, starting with the south half and gradually extending it to the north,

---

46 Capart 1936, 409-430; quotation on page 409.
47 Appendix II, letter no. **9**.
48 Wilson 1964, 102, is probably exaggerating the character of the relationship between the two men, stressing how poor Insinger was (though in comparison to Wilbour everybody must have appeared to be poor). One look at the house Insinger built for himself in Luxor (see below) will prove how unfounded the remark really is that he was 'eking out a living'.
49 Dates mentioned in three columns in *Het Nieuws van den Dag* of 5 September, 14 October, and 14 November 1887.
50 Capart 1936, 431-467.
51 Capart 1936, 463.
52 *Loc.cit.*; quoted also by Wilson 1964, 102.
53 Appendix II, letters nos. **12-14**; *Het Nieuws van den Dag*, 15 August 1888.
54 *Het Nieuws van den Dag*, 26 November 1888.

55 Capart 1936, 474-534; quotation on page 477.
56 *Ibid.* 502-503.
57 *Ibid.* 534.
58 *Ibid.* 547 (25 January, 1890).
59 Now RMO Archives, 19.19/1.
60 For the latter, see http://www.tawy.nl/insinger-house.html (accessed on 20 January, 2014).
61 For an aerial view, see http://nickyvandebeek.com/2014/05/insinger/ (accessed on 26 October 2016).
62 Son of Ismail Pasha, and ruler of Egypt from 1914-1917. See Carstens 1914, 340.
63 Quoted in translation on the website http://www.tawy.nl/insinger-house.html.

Fig. I.6. Exterior of Insinger's house in Luxor. Reproduction in the archives of the RMO.

where the grounds were closed off by a monumental gateway copied after the famous Puerta del Sol of Toledo. From there the house stretched along the Nile as a two-storied folly in Moorish style, its crenelated exterior walls striped in red and white and relieved by ogival window-frames, the corners strengthened by little turrets, and with a central tower modelled after the Palazzo Vecchio of Florence.[64] The land side offered a rather closed aspect, the Nile side was more open and had a distribution of several wings around a terraced garden on the river bank. Photographs of the interior show long corridors of which the walls are adorned with trophies of Islamic weapons and decorative ceramic plates and pictures, with large rooms furnished in Oriental style. The house was called *Palmenburg*, a pun on the Insinger family summerhouse of *Pijnenburg* in the Netherlands, whereas Insinger himself also referred to his residence as the 'Anti-Cook Hotel'.

Here Wilbour again visited in February 1891, noting that the house and the daughters had grown, and that Insinger was considerably less melancholic than in November of the previous year, when he was mourning the recent death of his sister-in-law Yasmeen.[65] Insinger was now a land-owner, living of the lease of his 15 acres and also acting as a money-lender and antiquities dealer (though the extent of the latter activity will be questioned below). Besides, he liked to entertain guests, and Wilbour commemorates a pleasant dinner which he enjoyed in the splendid house in the company of the archaeologists

Fig. I.7. Family portrait with the newborn son. Reproduction in the archives of the RMO.

Grébaut, Sayce, and Bouriant.[66] Unfortunately, this is the last time he mentions Insinger in his letters; the Wilbour Library in Brooklyn preserves six letters written by Insinger to his friend Wilbour (*abu dakn* = Arabic 'father of the beard') between 1893 and 1896, but these do not provide much information.[67] It is mentioned there that Insinger bought more land behind the house, planning to turn it into a public park, and was continuously improving the building. Another important event which took place during these years was the birth of Insinger's son and heir in 1892 (Fig. I.7). Because of Wilbour's death five years later we have to look elsewhere for information on the following period.

Insinger did not contact the RMO in Leiden again until after Leemans was pensioned in 1891. Perhaps he

---

64 Thereby the house was in the same style as the fashionable Hotel du Nil, established in 1836 at the crossing of Sharieh el-Muski and the Khalig Canal in Cairo, and closed in 1906.
65 Capart 1936, 571, 586.
66 Bierbrier 2012, 223, 489-490 and 75, respectively. Eugène Grébaut (1846-1915) was Maspero's successor as Director of the Antiquities Service from 1886 to 1892. Archibald Sayce (1845-1933) was Oxford professor of Assyriology and visited Egypt almost every winter. Urbain Bouriant (1849-1903) started his career as assistant curator at the Bulaq Museum and became Director of the Institut Français d'Archéologie Orientale in Cairo from 1886 to 1898.
67 I thank Rob J. Demarée for showing me a transcript of these letters, which mainly contain advice to Wilbour about the best way to get his boat repaired.

had given up all hopes that the stubborn director would ever purchase antiquities that were on offer in Egypt, and had therefore interrupted the correspondence of previous years. When Pleyte became successor to the director's post, Insinger soon resumed contact, announcing the dispatch of more photographs for the museum archives and asking to be sent a list of antiquities wanted by the RMO.[68] Pleyte was very eager to comply with this request, and as a result of this several interesting collections could be acquired during his directorship, which we shall discuss in the following chapter. Foremost was of course the acquisition of the famous Papyrus Insinger, which took from January to May 1895. After the safe arrival of the manuscript in the Leiden museum, Insinger communicated his intention to come to the Netherlands, his first visit since 16 years.[69] He wanted to see his two eldest daughters, who were now at school in Holland, and he needed some medical advice for himself and his wife. In spite of many other obligations, he also reserved some time for a visit to Leiden, where he finally met Pleyte in person on August 10th, after having corresponded with him for over 13 years.

The two men became real friends, and accordingly the tone of the succeeding letters became distinctly less formal. In a letter of August 2, 1896, Insinger still referred to their common meal in Leiden one year before, and invited Pleyte to come to Egypt.[70] However, the latter proposed to postpone the travel plans to 1898 because of private circumstances,[71] and then ill health prevented him from ever realizing this project. Insinger visited Holland a second time in July 1898, but missed Pleyte in Leiden and suffered so much from the climate that he swore never to come again.[72] News about his health problems now was a regular feature of his letters. Even so, these years were extremely productive as far as additions to the Leiden collections were concerned, and there was a steady stream of letters between the two gentlemen in order to organize the resulting acquisitions and shipments. In the summer of 1901, Insinger stayed for a month in Pallanza in Italy,[73] while one of his daughters visited the RMO in Leiden and was guided through the collections by the new curator, the Egyptologist Pieter Boeser; Pleyte was in hospital at the time for surgery to his feet.[74] In the end, it was Pleyte who would die two years later, whereas Insinger survived for almost two more decades.

5. Grumpy old man (1903-1918)

With Pleyte's death we lose yet another source of information on Insinger's life. Boeser occasionally kept up the correspondence until 1909, but no further transactions took place between Insinger and the RMO. For the first time in its history, the museum had a non-Egyptologist as its director: the classical archaeologist A.E.J. Holwerda (1845-1922). Though Boeser now acted as vice-director, the museum's attention clearly shifted to other fields of interest, and the growth of the Egyptian collections slacked noticeably. Thus the opportunity to make further use of Insinger's services for acquiring antiquities at a very reasonable price was missed. This seems to have added to the mounting feelings of frustration of the Dutchman, whose self-sought exile in Luxor gradually cut him off from the world that he had so enjoyed during his earlier years in Egypt. One of the factors which contributed to his sense of displacement was the growing influence of the British in the country.

Above, we have already sketched the political developments of the 1880s. Although it is very unlikely that the British intended a long-term occupation of Egypt, following the bombardment of Alexandria in 1882, their Consul-General Lord Cromer soon understood that the establishment of political stability was only one side of the matter.[75] Thus the British administration re-instated Tewfik Pasha in power as titular ruler of the country, under the suzerainty of the Turkish Sultan as before.[76] The British also started upon an ambitious project to reform the country's economy, which became increasingly dependent upon the cultivation of cotton, with the ensuing necessity to guarantee a continuous supply of irrigation water. To this effect, dams and dikes were built all over Egypt, and Nubia started drowning on a yearly basis by the construction of the first Aswan dam. The British also convinced Tewfik to yield the Sudan to the Mahdist revolt. It was not until 1896, under Tewfik's son and successor Abbas II, that a joint Egyptian-British force succeeded in suppressing the rebellion and regaining the country. Clearly, the British arms were there to stay. Thus the world as Insinger knew it was rapidly changing.

The Insingers themselves were distinctly French-oriented, spoke French at home, and were very close to the representatives of the *Service des Antiquités*, where French employees still dominated ever since the days of Mariette, and of the *Institut Français d'Archéologie Orientale*, which had been founded in Cairo in 1880. Having lived along

---

68 Appendix II, letters nos. **15-16**.
69 Appendix II, letter no. **26**.
70 Appendix II, letter no. **29**.
71 Archives RMO, dispatched letters 1896/169 of August 28.
72 Appendix II, letter no. **37**.
73 Appendix II, letter no. **51**.
74 Archives RMO, dispatched letters 1901/169 of July 29. Pleyte is said to have undergone the amputation of some toes, probably to alleviate the effects of his rheumatism (see Hasselbach 1987, 94); there is also an allusion to kidney problems (Appendix II, letter no. **49**).

75 For Cromer, see Carstens 1914, 183-184.
76 For Tewfik, see *ibid*. 657-658.

the Nile for several decades, they also identified themselves with the fate of the native population, among whom they had made many friends. Inevitably, they became more and more anti-English as time went by, and a family tradition has it that above the gate leading into Palmenburg there was an Arabic inscription reading 'May Allah preserve this house from the plague and from the Englishman'. Both in his Sudanese travel report and in his columns written for *Het Nieuws van den Dag*, Insinger is very critical of the British rule, and he ends his last contribution to the newspaper (about the ineffectual water regime) with the poignant exclamation 'Sed Carthaginem esse delendam. Beat the English to death!'[77] It is also in this context that we have to understand the jocular designation of the house as the 'Anti-Cook Hotel'.

All this did not help to make Insinger's last years any more pleasant. According to some sources, he tried to set himself up as an independent dealer in antiquities. He had never experienced many problems with the French administration of the *Service*, but soon he noticed that here, too, British politics were taking over. Thus from 1886 onwards the keeper of Egyptology of the British Museum, Ernest Wallis Budge (1857-1934),[78] used to visit Egypt every winter in order to hunt for antiquities, spoiling the market with the high prices offered by him to the local dealers at Luxor and elsewhere.[79] Insinger had the distinct feeling that this competition was only possible due to the direct protection by the British commissioners, and recounted with evident satisfaction how he had helped the Belgian Egyptologist Jean Capart (who was buying for the Brussels Museum) to appropriate some objects already fancied by Budge.[80] In the summer of 1903 this led to a serious clash with Howard Carter, just appointed as Chief Inspector of the antiquities of Upper Egypt and the future excavator of the tomb of Tutankhamun.[81] In a letter sent to the newspaper *Le Phare d'Alexandrie*, Insinger blamed Carter and Budge (though wisely identified as X and Y only) to have cooperated in the illicit shipment of a stela destined for the British Museum, adding that Carter had given other proofs of his incompetence. However, two days later *The Egyptian Gazette* published an editorial letter, taking a more balanced view on the matter and retaliating: 'In view of Mr. Insinger's peculiar position in Luxor we can also understand that an active and energetic Inspector like Mr. Carter is a considerable thorn in the flesh to him, and that such accusations as are brought against the latter, are prompted by a whole-souled desire to see the last of him.' Thus the accusation bounced back on Insinger, and this matter can hardly have contributed to his reputation in Luxor.

At the same time Insinger estranged himself from his few compatriots in Egypt by meddling in the affairs of the Dutch consulate in Cairo. It had been transferred there from Alexandria in 1884, and on that occasion the former consul-general Anslijn was replaced by a new one, Mr P.J.F.M. van der Does de Willebois.[82] When in 1906 a new consular agent had to be appointed, Van der Does suggested the son-in-law of the former incumbent, who happened to be German by birth. Immediately Insinger sent an indignant letter to the newspaper *Nieuwe Rotterdamsche Courant*, protesting that a foreigner should not be considered suitable for such a post. When consulted about the matter, Van der Does wrote about Insinger to the Secretary of Foreign Affairs: 'Those who know this person, who is notorious as one of the worst and most unscrupulous usurers in Egypt, will be struck by his highly peculiar performance as champion of the offended national feelings.'[83]

Obviously, Insinger slowly became a grumpy old man, a circumstance to which his own declining health and the frequent mental depressions of his wife will certainly have contributed. Fortunately, his eldest daughter returned to Egypt with her husband, the merchant Carl Iversen who worked for the Insinger firm, and the couple even settled in Luxor for some time.[84] This will have relieved the increasing isolation of the elderly couple in their large house. In 1911, Insinger lost his father; he will have found pleasure in the fact that the old man legated his house Pijnenburg to his grand-son, Insinger's own son Edmond, who adapted it for permanent habitation. The outbreak of the First World War brought further tensions. Because of his sympathy for the Central Powers, Abbas II was deposed by the British military authorities in 1914 and the Khedivate of Egypt thereby ended.[85] Instead, Abbas's uncle Hussein Kamel was appointed as Sultan of Egypt, to rule independently of the Ottoman Empire though under British protection. In Luxor, these events meant the

---

77 *Het Nieuws van den Dag*, 12 February 1894.
78 Bierbrier 2012, 90-92; Thompson 2015, 166-170; for Budge's acquisition policy, see James 1981, 23-25.
79 Appendix II, letter no. **51**.
80 Appendix II, letter no. **49**. For Capart (1877-1947), see Bierbrier 2012, 103-104.
81 For Carter (1874-1939), see Bierbrier 2012, 105-106, who notes that he held the position of inspector for Upper Egypt from 1899 to 1904, then moving to the inspectorate of Lower Egypt where he resigned one year later due to a conflict about some French tourists (*cf*. Thompson 2015, 112-114). For the following episode, see Budge 1920, 364-367; Wilson 1964, 129-130; and more fully James 1992, 76-79. The stela in question is that of Tjetji (now British Museum EA 614).

82 Algemeen Rijksarchief (National Archives), The Hague, Correspondence with the diplomatic office in Egypt and the general consulate at Alexandria, 1861-1884, 2.05.38/1497.
83 *Ibid.*, letter of 5 April 1906.
84 *Nederland's Patriciaat* 72 (1988), 272.
85 For Abbas, see Carstens 2014, 3-4.

Fig. I.8. Insinger's tomb at Lage Vuursche. Photo in RMO Archives.

end of tourism, though not – surprisingly – of archaeological fieldwork, since Insinger's former opponent Carter was back in the Valley of the Kings.[86]

One of Insinger's old friends at least kept turning up at the Anti-Cook Hotel: his fellow consumptive Archibald Sayce from Oxford. In his *Reminiscences*,[87] Sayce describes how he arrived in Luxor in March 1918, where everything was closed due to the war except for the Luxor Hotel which swarmed with British soldiers. He passed a pleasant day on the Nile with Insinger in his steamer, 'little thinking that I should see him no more.' Indeed, arriving in Cairo for his next season in Egypt in October of the same year, he received sad news about his friend: 'I had not been long in Cairo before I received a great shock, Insinger's son-in-law, who was a resident there, telling me that his father-in-law had been seized with a sudden attack of illness and had just been brought to the English hospital on the Gezira [= the island in the Nile at Cairo]. I promised to call on him the following morning, but before I could do so news was brought to me that he was dead, and I attended his funeral the next day.' Insinger died on 27 October, 1918. His body was transferred to the Netherlands, where it was buried on the cemetery of the village of Lage Vuursche, close to the family house of Pijnenburg where he had spent part of his youth and where his son now lived. Later, a funerary monument in Egyptian design was erected over the burial (Fig. I.8), consisting of a sarcophagus with gabled lid backed by a rectangular stela with cavetto cornice, the latter flanked by lower side-wings, and with low railings around the whole. The stela is blank, but there is a short inscription on the foot-end of the sarcophagus. The latter has Egyptianising reliefs on the lateral walls, each depicting a kneeling officiant facing a papyrus bush, the one on the left holding a lotus over the rear shoulder and stretching the other arm forward, the other raising a finger to the lips and with the rear arm down.

After Insinger's death, the splendid house in Luxor was vacated and soon came into the hands of the khedivial family, who used it as a summer residence. We assume that Insinger's wife and children will also have left Egypt, taking with them some of the antiquities and other valuables that may have been left. Insinger's wife Mariam would live on till 1941, when she died in a mental institution in Vevey (Switzerland). Other descendants also settled in the Netherlands, as we shall see in the next section, and later also in Canada.

---

86   James 1992, 167-190.
87   Sayce 1923, 453, 457.

Chapter II

Jan Herman Insinger as a purveyor of antiquities for the RMO

1. Exploits with Schelling (1882)

Previous publications have mainly highlighted the person of Insinger as a traveller[1] and photographer.[2] In the following, I shall endeavour to sketch an image of this fascinating personality as a dealer in antiquities, especially in his contacts with the Leiden Museum. It is hardly an exaggeration to state that without this precious lifeline between the RMO and the land of Egypt, the growth of the Egyptian collections would have known a much slower pace during the years 1880-1920. Moreover, Insinger was responsible for filling a number of obvious lacunas in the Egyptian holdings of the museum, a notable feat which was performed without him knowing the collections from personal inspection: he never visited the Netherlands between 1879 and 1895, and only developed his interest in the pharaonic heritage after his arrival in Egypt.

In fact, we can pinpoint his first encounter with archaeological finds to the year 1882, when he made his afore-mentioned camel trip to the Oasis Kurkur in the company of Antonie Schelling. The latter travelled with a written authorization signed by Serrurier, Director of the National Ethnographic Museum in Leiden, and permitting him to buy objects for account of the said museum to a maximum value of 500 Dutch guilders. This permit is explicitly mentioned in a letter written by Schelling to Serrurier after his return to Cairo.[3] Here he explains that he already sent a box full of objects to Leiden, most of them for the Ethnographic Museum but including some finds destined as a donation to the Museum of Antiquities, which should accordingly be handed over to Pleyte. It is not clear whether Insinger was personally involved in these archaeological finds, though Schelling states that several of the ethnographic objects had in fact been given him by his travel companion. The least we can say is that the finds were probably made in Insinger's presence. The list of antiquities given in the letter runs as follows:

a red pottery water vessel with very thin walls, and a ditto bowl with rather narrow bottom and thick walls, both from Quft, located about one day downstream from Luxor and on the same bank; 1 red pottery jar with narrow neck and 2 handles, and 1 other ditto of white pottery without handles and without foot, both from Wallad e'Sheikh diagonally opposite Girgeh; inscribed potsherds from Karnak; several chopped flints, picked up by me on the plateau on which the monastery Mar Girgis Katl e'Taniel is situated, between Menshiyeh and Akhmim and on the right-hand bank. There were numerous flints weapons here, so that we just had to pick them up. Finally a ribbed pot

---

1 Insinger 2004.
2 Raven 1991; Raven 2009.
3 National Museum of Ethnology, Leiden, Archives, letter of Schelling to Serrurier, 1 June 1882.

Fig. II.1. RMO inv.no. AES 1: fragmentary amphora, Coptic period, h. 47 cm.

Fig. II.2. RMO inv.no. AES 5: amphora, Coptic period, h. 38 cm.

Fig. II.3. RMO inv.no. AES 8: limestone stela of Sebekhotep, New Kingdom, h. 33, w. 28 cm.

Fig. II.4. RMO inv.no. AES 7: limestone stela of Herunefer and Beshau, 18th Dynasty, h. 49, w. 33 cm.

Fig. II.5. RMO inv.no. AES 7: serpentine bowl, Early Dynastic period, h. 8 cm.

of red pottery, partly broken but with the sherds added. On a desert trip meant to trace a temple situated there according to our guide (but which was not there), we arrived on the 2nd day at a mountain range: Jebel Garra. During our explorations, while we were climbing up several times, I found this vessel at more than mid-height in the same condition as I send it, with next to it the fragments which have been added here and which join. A second, similar vessel but utterly smashed lay a couple of metres lower.

The objects were duly taken over by the RMO on 7 July 1882 and were registered as inventory numbers AES 1-6: no. 1 for the pot from Jebel Garra (Fig. II.1),[4] nos. 2 and 3 for those from Awlad el-Sheikh,[5] nos. 5 and 4 for the pots from Quft (Fig. II.2), and no. 6 for the flint implements from Mari Girgis.[6] The pottery all dates to the Coptic period. AES 6 is a collection of 54 dark brown flints, only partly worked but to a large extent formed by nature, as was already demonstrated by Professor U. Fischer from Freiburg, who examined the flints later in 1882.[7] Leemans reported that the ostraca from Karnak had not arrived, and Schelling could only conclude that they might have been stolen and promised to ask Insinger to send others.[8]

In the meantime, Insinger himself had already written to Pleyte from Italy, where he was spending the summer, announcing the transport of another batch of antiquities: a small stela bought by Schelling at el-Kab (Fig. II.3) and a larger one bought by himself

---

4   The 547 m high Jebel Garra lies due west of Aswan at 24°3' north and 32°31' east.
5   Small village on the east bank, a bit to the north of Girga. Schelling provides a sketch of this site in his letter to Leemans of 5 december 1882 (Archives RMO, letters received, 1882/242).
6   For this monastery and its location just east of Akhmim, see Henein 1988. The rest of the toponym is unknown (the first element is probably to be understood as Arabic *kafr* = village, hamlet). Again there is a sketch of the situation in Schelling's letter (see previous footnote).
7   Apart from the 54 items, there are four others from the Schelling donation (AEF 7-10) which were used to strike fire, according to Fischer, and are now kept separately. See RMO inventory books, no. 12, page 11. For correspondence on the Schelling donation, see RMO Archives, letters received 1882/97, 101; letters dispatched 1882/136-137, 142, 146.
8   Archives RMO, letters dispatched, 1882/324; letters received, 1882/243.

in Thebes but probably originally from Abydos (Fig. II.4).[9] Upon arrival, the donation proved to include an Early Dynastic serpentine bowl picked up by Schelling in Awlad el-Sheikh as well (Fig. II.5);[10] the objects received inventory numbers AES 7-9. The larger stela was originally put up by two majors of Memphis of the early New Kingdom, probably at the Osiris temple of Abydos.[11] The other (smaller) one has a very rough carving which has probably been retouched by a modern dealer. Insinger mentions the latter was shown to Maspero, who already suspected a Roman period recarving. Maspero was also said to be jealous of the archaic bowl, because the Bulaq Museum did not yet possess a complete specimen at the time, but apparently this was no ground to stop the object from being exported.

2. Manuscripts and mummies (1886)

At the beginning of 1883 Schelling was very worried about the health of Insinger, who was then in Wadi Halfa, suffering from stomach problems and awaiting a doctor.[12] He cannot have suspected that in fact he himself would be dead within three months, at the age of 29, whereas his friend would survive for another 35 years.[13] Schelling left a small collection of objects behind, which were sent to the Leiden Museum of Ethnography by his brother (P. Schelling in Gouda), and from there the antiquities were delivered to the RMO.[14] Because there is no evidence that Insinger was involved in their acquisition, they will not be dealt with here. Insinger did not bring any antiquities from his Sudan trip (though he supplied some ethnographical objects to the Leiden Museum of Ethnography[15]), and he did not contact the RMO until 1884, with the offer to act as intermediary in the sale of a collection of textile samples made by Emil Brugsch. Obviously, Insinger was quite aware of the clandestine character of this transaction, which presented a marked contrast with his own frank behaviour regarding the 1882 export of antiquities, for which he had taken the trouble to consult Maspero. Probably he was quite relieved to hear that Leemans considered the price too high, so that the offer was declined.[16] Of course this may have been a polite way of evading the awkward point of the legitimacy of the purchase, though we cannot prove whether this aspect was considered.

The next contact occurred at the very end of 1885, when Insinger wrote a letter from el-Balyana (near the site of Abydos) in Upper Egypt.[17] Here he mentioned that he had just acquired a collection of about 120 Coptic manuscripts, which he offered to sell to the museum for no more than the average price of acquisition. Because he added that some of the manuscripts had been inspected by Maspero and others had even been translated by Bouriant (assistant curator at the Bulaq Museum), Leemans must have felt comfortable about the transaction and the purchase was made. The manuscripts arrived in Leiden

---

9 Appendix II, letter no. **1**.
10 Appendix II, letter no. **2**.
11 Gessler-Löhr 1997, 31-34 and Taf. 1. It should be corrected that this is the specimen bought at Thebes, not the one from el-Kab as stated *ibid*. 32, n. 8 (the confusion stems from the incorrect registration in the RMO inventory book, no. 12, page 13).
12 This is mentioned in his letter to Serrurier of February 14; see above, p. 14 n. 22.
13 An obituary of Schelling was published by the Dutch Geographical Society, of which Schelling was a corresponding member (communication by Saskia Asser). A photograph taken by Insinger and now in an album kept at Amsterdam University Library (no. 1334 A 25, photo 6) shows Schelling's tomb-stone on the English cemetery in Old-Cairo, inscribed 'Antonie Johannes Schelling / ingenieur neerlandais / né 18 Septembre 1854 / mort 3 May 1883 / Dieu l'a appelé'. Later, his remains were transferred to the cemetery of Ouderkerk aan den IJssel, where they lie under a broken column (see Stenvert 2004, sub Ouderkerk aan den IJssel).
14 Inv.nos. AES 10-39, acquired in 1884. See RMO Archives, letters received 1884/120, 125; letters dispatched 1884/141-142, 149.
15 Some of these are illustrated in Insinger 2004, figs. 23, 29, 37-39.
16 Appendix II, letter no. **3**; RMO Archives, letters dispatched 1884/112.
17 Appendix II, letter no. **4**.

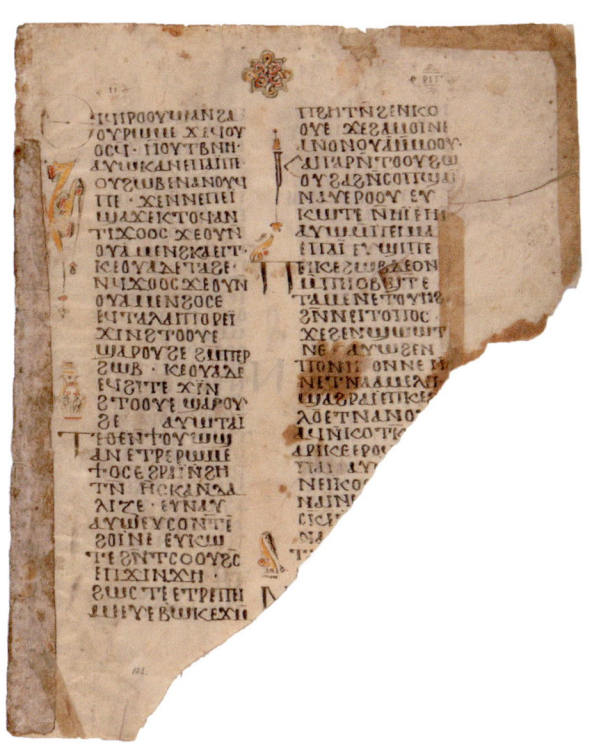

Fig. II.6. RMO inv.no. AES 40-1, sheet 1 recto: rules for monastic life, Coptic period, h. 34.3, w. 28.2 cm.

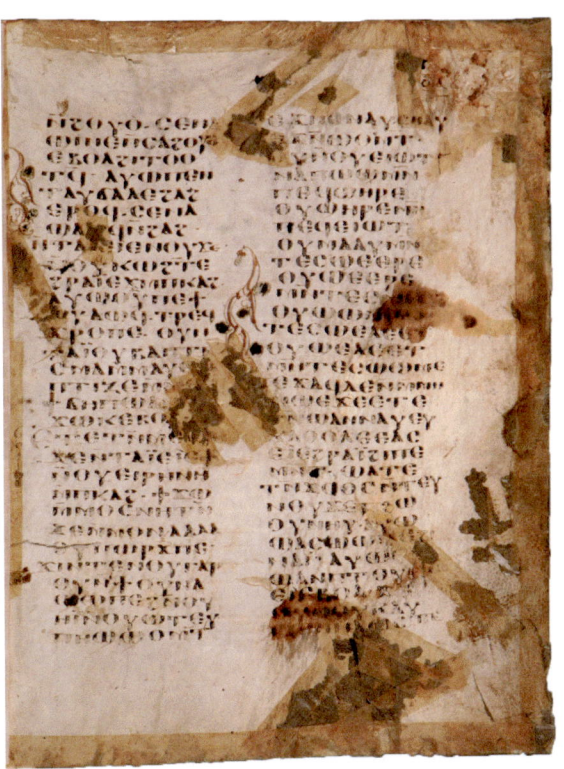

Fig. II.7. RMO inv.no. AES 40-13, sheet 2 recto: Gospel of St. Luke, Coptic period, h. 26.2, w. 21.1 cm.

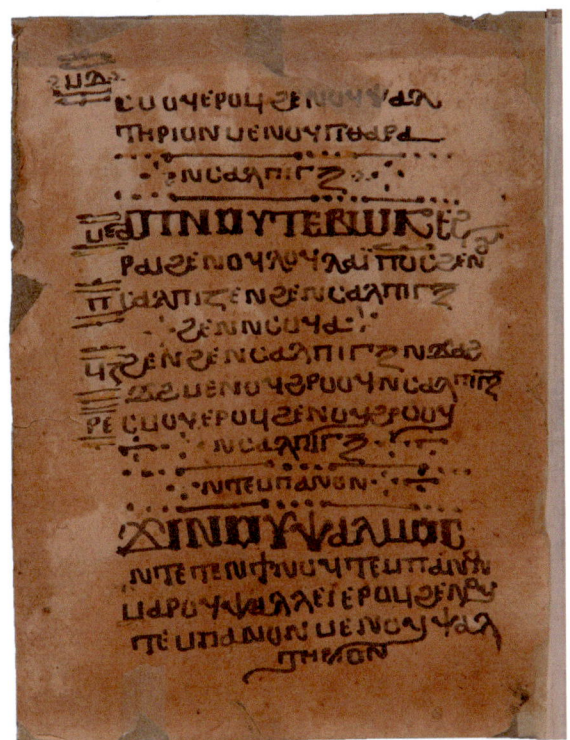

Fig. II.8. RMO inv.no. AES 40-24, page 2 verso: index on the Psalms, Coptic period, h. 18, w. 15.5 cm.

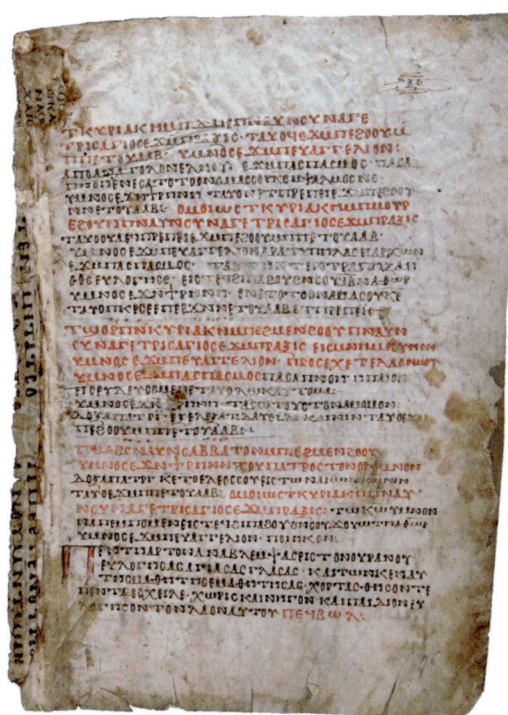

Fig. II.9. RMO inv.no. AES 40-44, recto: antiphonarium, Coptic period, h. 31.6, w. 23.5 cm.

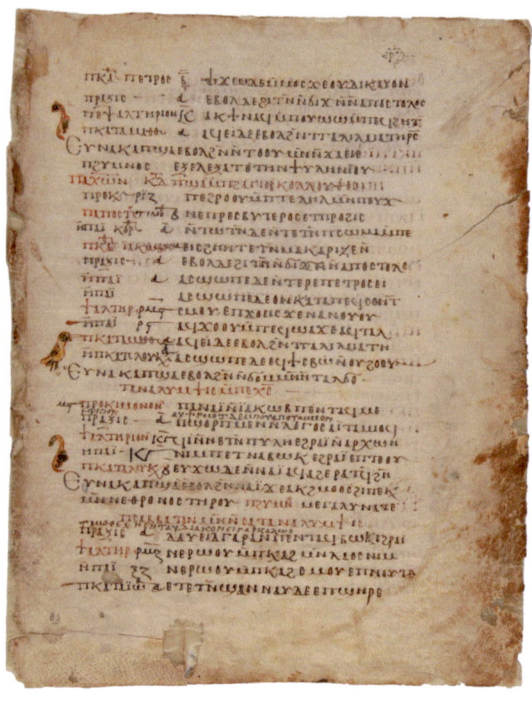

Fig. II.10. RMO inv.no. AES 40-53, recto: index on Bible texts, Coptic period, h. 33, w. 26.5 cm.

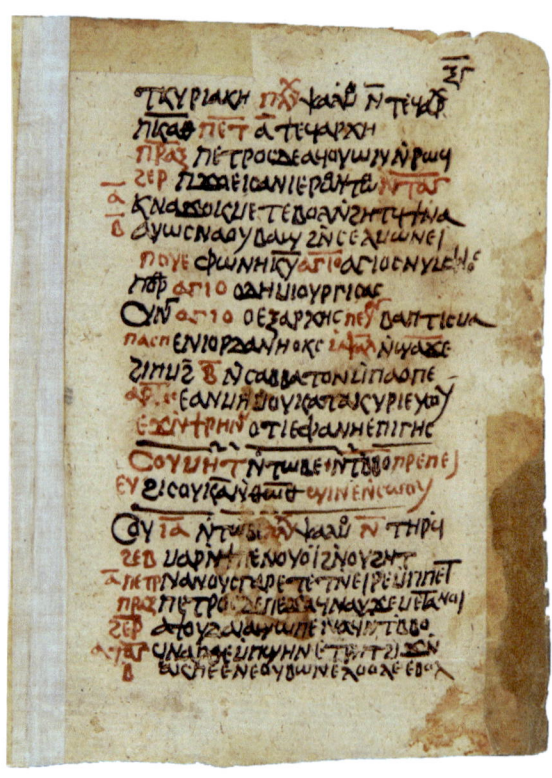

Fig. II.11. RMO inv.no. AES 40-56, page 1: list of Biblical passages, Coptic period, h. 17.2, w. 12.5 cm.

Fig. II.12. RMO inv.no. AES 40-59, page 1: liturgy, Coptic period, h. 17.5, w. 13.6 cm.

Fig. II.13. RMO inv.no. AES 40-91, recto: sermon on the expulsion of the devil, Coptic period, h. 31.4, w. 25.2 cm.

with some delay (Figs. II.6-13), because they had been sent via Insinger's brother Willem Alexander who lived in a villa in Baarn (near the family house Pijnenburg).[18] One of the conditions of the sale was that the museum would take care of their speedy publication, a condition Leemans was reluctant to meet because there were no specialists of Coptic in the Netherlands at the time. However, Pleyte was already instructing Pieter Boeser (who had a degree in Dutch literature) in the principles of the Egyptian language, and afterwards the young scholar spent some years with Erman and Steindorff in Germany. When he returned to Leiden, it was as an able philologist, and after some volunteer work at the museum Boeser was appointed as curator in 1892.[19] One of the first tasks he undertook was the study of the Insinger manuscripts, and this led to the admirable publication *Manuscrits coptes* five years later.[20]

In his letters, Insinger never mentions where and how he acquired the manuscripts in question. More information is given in the introduction to the *Manuscrits coptes*.[21] Here it is stated that in 1883 Maspero himself rediscovered a secret closet in the monastery of Amba Shenuda near Akhmim (better known as the White Monastery of Sohag)[22] where the monks used to store their ancient manuscripts. This had already been partially plundered at the end of the 18th century, but had then allegedly been forgotten for about a hundred years. This is the story that Maspero himself liked to tell, and that he published in almost the same words in his introduction to a publication on the manuscripts acquired from the same source by the Bibliothèque Nationale in Paris.[23] However, it has since become clear that in fact the presence of the secret chamber was known to the local population ever since about 1778, and that they had been selling isolated pages for over a century already before the source was 'rediscovered'.[24] Moreover, the Paris manuscripts were only purchased (by the exertions of Maspero himself) in four lots between March 1886 and October 1887, leaving an unexplained delay between the alleged moment of discovery and that of acquisition. It has since been questioned whether the date of 1883 is in fact correct, and on the basis of a note in pencil inscribed by Amélineau in his personal copy of the *Manuscrits coptes* we can be fairly sure that it was Amélineau (not Maspero) who first entered the secret room in the monastery, and that this happened in 1885 (with Maspero's inspection taking place in 1886).[25] We can suspect that Insinger had just bought his share of the plunder from one of the local dealers at Akhmim when he wrote his letter from Balyana, 50 km further south.[26] Thus his acquisition must have preceded Maspero's visit, and may almost have coincided with Amélineau's. Though Maspero could save about 3,800 sheets for the Bibliothèque Nationale, quite a lot of other manuscripts had already been appropriated by local dealers in the meantime, which ended up in collections in Paris, Berlin, London, and elsewhere.[27] By 1892, the closet was said to be empty.[28]

In a letter to Insinger of 24 December, 1885, Leemans explicitly mentions that he would like to continue buying excavated material, provided this could be exported by official permission of Maspero and the Bulaq Museum.[29] For Insinger, this opened up the prospect of earning some money with the antiquities trade, though he does not seem to have gained anything on the transaction of the Coptic manuscripts if we may believe his letters to Leemans.[30] Accordingly, he again contacted the RMO director on 21 March, 1886, having arrived in Assiut after his trip to the south.[31] He reported the purchase of two mummies, freshly uncovered at the excavations at Akhmim and sold to him by Maspero in person. Insinger offered to send these to Leiden, again for no more than the nominal costs. Leemans was slow in reacting, and made

---

18 Inv.no. AES 40. See Appendix II, letters nos. **4-5**; RMO Archives, letters received 1886/11, 70; letters dispatched 1885/201, 1886/55, 93, 95, 100.
19 Van Wijngaarden 1935, 15-17.
20 Pleyte/Boeser 1897. Van Wijngaarden 1935, 17 confirms that the major work was done by Boeser.
21 Pleyte/Boeser 1897, v-vi.
22 Insinger himself had guessed the manuscripts were from the Red Monastery instead; see Appendix II, letter no. **4**.
23 Maspero 1892, 1-2.
24 Hyvernat 1933, 105-107. The last purchase antedating the 'rediscovery' mentioned there dates to 1863 (107 n. 4), so at most there was an interval of twenty years during which the closet was 'lost'.

25 *Ibid.*, 107-109. For Émile Amélineau (1850-1915), who was a student of Maspero and worked with the French archaeological mission in Egypt from 1883-1887, see Bierbrier 2012, 17.
26 For these dealers, see Baedeker 1891, 57. Probably, these involved the Ledid brothers, but the French consul Frénay was also involved in the sales: see Hagen/Ryholt 2016, 197 and 216 with further reference to the Akhmim manuscripts.
27 Maspero may have been inspecting the excavations at nearby Akhmim at the moment Insinger wrote his letter from el-Balyana, because he states that he showed some of his manuscripts to Maspero, who was much interested. Thus, it may even have been Insinger who alerted Maspero about the find at Sohag. More manuscripts could be bought locally as late as March 1886 (Appendix II, letter no. **6**), but in the meantime the prices had already gone up due to stiff competition between the various museums and their agents. For a more detailed report on the library and its dispersal, see M. Krause, in: Atiya 1991, vol. 5, 1447-1450 s.v. *Libraries*.
28 Maspero 1892, 2. *Cf.* Baedeker 1898, 207.
29 RMO Archives, dispatched letter 1885/201.
30 Appendix II, letter no. **5**. Also, later letters imply that he was only asking the RMO to be reimbursed for the costs of acquisition and transport, and was not making any profit himself. See below, Chapter III, §12.
31 Appendix II, letter no. **6**.

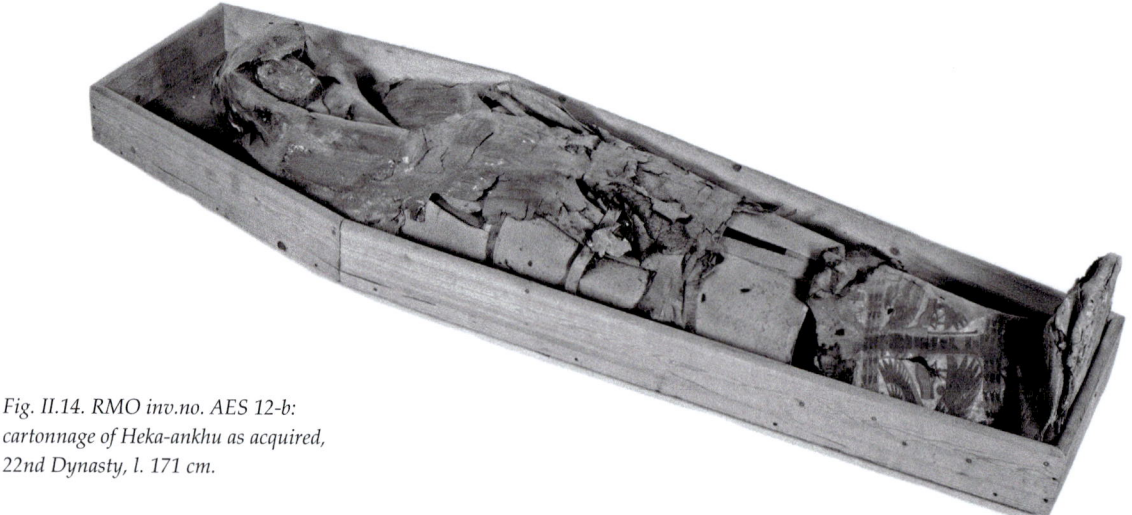

Fig. II.14. RMO inv.no. AES 12-b: cartonnage of Heka-ankhu as acquired, 22nd Dynasty, l. 171 cm.

an awkward endeavour to involve also the Dutch judge Adrianus Heemskerk[32] in his plans to buy mummies: the son of the Home Secretary, who was in Egypt that summer. Thus Insinger had to repeat his offer on 24 June, and only on July 15th Leemans confirmed his intention to make the deal.[33] The two mummies arrived in Leiden by the end of the year and were registered as inv.nos. AES 12-15 – a mistake, because these numbers had already been given to the objects of the Schelling legacy, so in the modern digitised registration '-a' has been added to the old Schelling numbers and '-b' to the objects purchased by Insinger from 1886 onwards.

All that is left of the first 'mummy' (AES 12-b) is a much decayed cartonnage of 22nd Dynasty type (Fig. II.14), which has been partly restored and cleaned recently (Fig. II.15). It was acquired together with a plain wooden coffin of the same date, provided with an inscription for a man called Heka-ankhu (AES 13-b, Fig. II.16). According to the inventory book there were a skull and some loose bones inside the cartonnage when it arrived in Leiden, but these cannot be found nowadays and may have been discarded. The second mummy (AES 14-b, Fig. II.17) is of regular Ptolemaic type, provided with polychrome cartonnage panels and a matching coffin (AES 15-b, Fig. II.18) inscribed for a woman Diptah.[34] It is very similar to another mummy and its coffin (AdS 1-2, inscribed for

Fig. II.15. RMO inv.no. AES 12-b: upper part of cartonnage of Heka-ankhu as restored, 22nd Dynasty, h. c. 50 cm.

---

32 Adrianus Heemskerk (1848-1908) was justice at the international court in Cairo and later judge in Amsterdam. See http://meervank.home.xs4all.nl/parenteel_heemskerk_053/parenteel_heemskerk_053.htm sub VII.23.2 (accessed 27-10-2016).

33 Appendix II, letter no. 7, with Leemans's answer preserved in the RMO Archives, Dispatched letters 1886/128.

34 For this mummy, see Raven/Taconis 2005, cat. 20.

Fig. II.16. (left) RMO inv.no. AES 13-b: coffin of Heka-ankhu, 22nd Dynasty, l. 184 cm.

Fig. II.17. (center) RMO inv.no. AES 14-b: mummy of Diptah, Ptolemaic period, l. 154.5 cm.

Fig. II.18. (right) RMO inv. no. AES 15-b: coffin of Diptah, Ptolemaic period, l. 174 cm.

a man Hor), donated to the RMO at the same time by Victor de Stuers, referendary at the Ministry of the Interior, who had received it via a friend in Egypt from the widow of a European official.[35] It is tempting to guess that this friend was the aforementioned Heemskerk, whose father (the Home Secretary) had appointed De Stuers. The coffin and mummy clearly display the local style of Akhmim, which is further evidence for the importance of this cemetery in the art market at the time.

The necropolis of Akhmim had been discovered by Maspero in 1884 near the monastery at el-Hawawish, to the north-east of the town.[36] Originally a cemetery of Old Kingdom rock tombs, the area was later extended with numerous caves, pits, and shafts filled with an estimate of 8,000-10,000 mummies of all periods, though mainly dating to the Graeco-Roman era. Insinger's letter indicates that Maspero was not excavating himself, leaving the job to local entrepreneurs who were entitled to half of their finds. A less favourable view was presented by Petrie, who visited the place in 1886 and asserted that 'a French Consul was put there (without any subjects to represent) and he raided and stripped the place under Consular seal which could not be interfered with'.[37] The consul in question was none other than the French mill-owner Auguste Frénay

---

35 For the provenance, see the note in the RMO inventory book, no. 14, page 23. For this mummy, see Raven/Taconis 2005, cat. 21. For De Stuers, see http://resources.huygens.knaw.nl/bwn1880-2000/lemmata/bwn1/stuers (accessed 28-10-2016).

36 For this find, see Maspero 1884, 66-68; Maspero 1886, 85-90; Baedeker 1891, 56-57. For the location, *cf.* Kanawati 1980, fig. 1.

37 Petrie 1931, 75. For William Matthew Flinders Petrie (1853-1942), see Bierbrier 2012, 428-430.

whom we shall meet again later with regard to the acquisition of the Papyrus Insinger.[38] As a result, thousands of mummies from Akhmim were transported to Cairo, practically without supervision, and many were then shipped to Europe.

3. Ostraca and textiles (1888)

In his letters written to Leemans from Cairo that summer, Insinger mentions that Maspero resigned from his position as Director of the Antiquities Service, and was succeeded by Eugène Grébaut.[39] The latter was a former pupil of Maspero, and had served as director of the French archeological institute in Cairo for the last three years.[40] Insinger hastened to make Grébaut's acquaintance and received the confirmation that, like his predecessor, he was willing to sell objects to Leemans, who – aged 77 but still acting director of the RMO – was by now regarded as the 'nestor of Egyptology'. Moreover, whereas Maspero only discussed selling doubles from recent excavations, Grébaut now proposed selling duplicates from the collections of the Cairo Museum itself – a controversial initiative about which Insinger (and doubtless many others at the time) seems to have felt some reserve. Thus, statues and stelae of Old Kingdom date and shabtis from the royal cache at Deir el-Bahari were explicitly mentioned. On the one hand, Leemans's reaction was to ask for a detailed list of what was on offer, but on the other he stated that Old Kingdom art in Leiden did not really form a lacuna (which was obviously untrue at the time, and it is still a weak section even today) and therefore dismissed the offer.[41] Financial considerations may have lain at the basis of this hesitant behaviour, but looking back on this episode one can only wonder why such splendid opportunities for enriching the Leiden collections were not used.

A better perspective was offered by Insinger's remark that he had acquired a number of textiles from the excavations at Akhmim, plus some others from the royal mummies which had been dissected earlier that summer in his presence.[42] He intended to send these to his brother in Baarn, together with a box with ostraca from Karnak and elsewhere, but it lasted until April 1888 before the

Fig. II.19. RMO inv.no. AES 19-b: vessel for a water wheel (qadus), Coptic period, h. 35 cm.

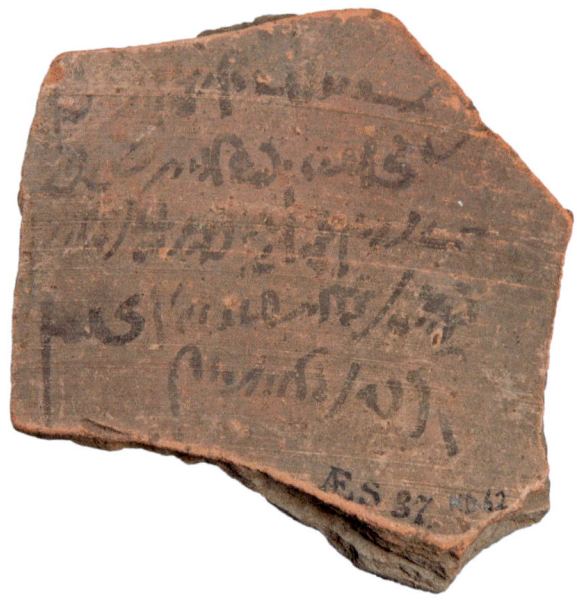

Fig. II.20. RMO inv.no. AES 37-b: demotic ostracon with a receipt for a payment of chaff, Roman period (23-24 AD), 6.2 x 7.4 cm.

---

38 Below, p. 35-36; Frénay is explicitly mentioned by Maspero 1887b, 216; see also Hagen/Ryholt 2016, 35, 216. According to Wilbour, the Akhmim dealer Ledid had three rooms full of mummies in 1886 (quoted by Hagen/Ryholt 2016, 197).
39 Appendix II, letters nos. **7-8**. For Grébaut, cf. Thompson 2015, 25-28.
40 Bierbrier 2012, 223. Maspero resigned in June and returned to France.
41 RMO Archives, letters dispatched, 1886/177 and 182 of October-November.
42 Appendix II, letter no. **8**. For the mummy dissections, see above, p. 16-17.

Fig. II.21. (above) RMO inv.no. AES 126: Greek ostracon with a receipt for poll tax, Roman period (3 AD), 10.3 x 8 cm.

Fig. II.22. (right) RMO inv.no. AES 155: detail of piled cloth comprising two tabulae depicting fruit and flowers, Coptic period (4th-5th century), 210 x 70.5 cm.

transport finally arrived in the museum. These finds were registered as nos. AES 16-b – 173 and proved to consist of six vessels of various periods (presumably also from Karnak; Fig. II.19), no less than 132 ostraca in Greek and demotic (most of them from Karnak, though the editors of these text suggest Koptos, Diospolis Magna, and Elephantine as the original provenance of some of them; Figs. II.20-21),[43] and 31 assorted textiles. Clearly, the ostraca were meant to form a compensation for the missing ostraca of the earlier donation of 1882. Ostraca were clearly not a category of objects much favoured by most contemporary archaeologists, and the Antiquities Service allowed native farmers looking for fertile soil (*sebakh*) from the ancient ruins to take them in huge quantities, which were then sold to the tourists. This practice is mentioned by several passing scholars,[44] and Insinger must have used the opportunity to form a large collection of ostraca himself, which was then sold to the RMO in several instalments. Most of this first lot seems to have come from the Karnak temple, where little boys roamed around looking for treasure while Maspero's workmen were slowly freeing the monument from the layers of debris accumulated over the ages.[45]

Regarding the textiles from the same shipment, most of these prove to date to the Coptic period, and derive from Akhmim (inv.nos. AES 155-159 and 162-172). Here the excavations had now moved to a sector of the necropolis which dated to the Graeco-Roman and Christian periods.[46] Among the burials were several of individuals who may have been attached to the local monastery, and most of them were richly dressed in ornamental clothing with decoration in tapestry technique (Figs. II.22-23). As a result, the whole cemetery was rifled by local art dealers and European travellers alike, but apparently this did not incite Maspero to organise proper supervision of the work, and his report of the plunder is very laconic. Recent research has shown that these textiles date to the

---

43 The demotic ostraca were published by Nur el-Din 1974, the Greek ones by Bagnall/Sijpesteijn/Worp 1980.
44 *Cf.* Sayce 1923, 211-212; Erman 1929, 219-220.
45 For a report on Maspero's work in Karnak and the find of extensive domestic structures there, see Maspero 1886, 49-56.
46 Maspero 1887b, 210-212. A reference to this trade in Akhmim textiles also occurs in Wilbour's letters: Capart 1936, 349; quoted in Van 't Hooft *et al.* 1994, 141.

4th to 9th centuries AD.⁴⁷ Somewhat earlier (1st-4th cent.) were three fragments of a tunic and sashes said to be from 'Terouth opposite Armant' (inv.nos. AES 160-161, Fig. II.24).⁴⁸ There can be no doubt that this garbled toponym refers to Tod, where Maspero was also conducting excavations from 1881 onwards. Apart from the remains of two temples, Tod also had a cemetery of the Christian period, when it served as a bishopric. This was explored especially from 1884 on, and contained a number of bodies dressed in ornamental textiles much like those at Akhmim.⁴⁹ Together, these two groups were the earliest Coptic textiles to arrive in the Egyptian collections in Leiden. The remaining textiles of this shipment concern some fragments of a bag-tunic found with the royal mummies in Deir el-Bahari (AES 154a-e) and several samples of unknown provenance (AES 173a-g).⁵⁰

Fig. II.23. (left) RMO inv.no. AES 167: fragment of cloth with U-shaped border and two medallions filled with interlacing motif, Coptic period (4th-5th century), 72 x 29 cm.

Fig. II.24. (right) RMO inv. no. AES 160-161: fragments of striped tunic and two sashes, Coptic period (1st-4th century), c. 135 x 135 cm.

4. Purchase of a papyrus (1895)

In the course of 1888 Insinger seems to have resumed addressing some of his letters to Pleyte,⁵¹ rather than to the stubborn Leemans who was obviously not interested in obtaining some of the duplicates of the Cairo Museum that Grébaut was selling.⁵² Accordingly, the letters mainly deal with the photographs of which Insinger was now sending prints for safekeeping in the museum's archives.⁵³ He seems to have given up

---

47 Van 't Hooft *et al.* 1994, especially 5 (on Insinger's activities) and 193 (concordance of registration numbers), cat.nos. 360-365, 368-370, 389, 422, 437, 442-443, 454.
48 *Ibid.* cat.nos. 357-359.
49 Maspero 1889a, 185-186.
50 Van 't Hooft *et al.* 1994, cat. nos. 90 and 473.
51 Appendix II, letters nos. **11** and **13**.
52 In a letter of 19 July 1888 Leemans stated that there was not much money available for the purchase of antiquities, yet on 10 August of the same year he asked for a detailed list of Grébaut's duplicates (RMO Archives, dispatched letters 1888/201 and 220). It is unknown whether such a list was sent, and this seems to mark an interruption of the correspondence that was to last more than five years.
53 Appendix II, letters nos. **8-14**. For Insinger's photographs, see Raven 1991.

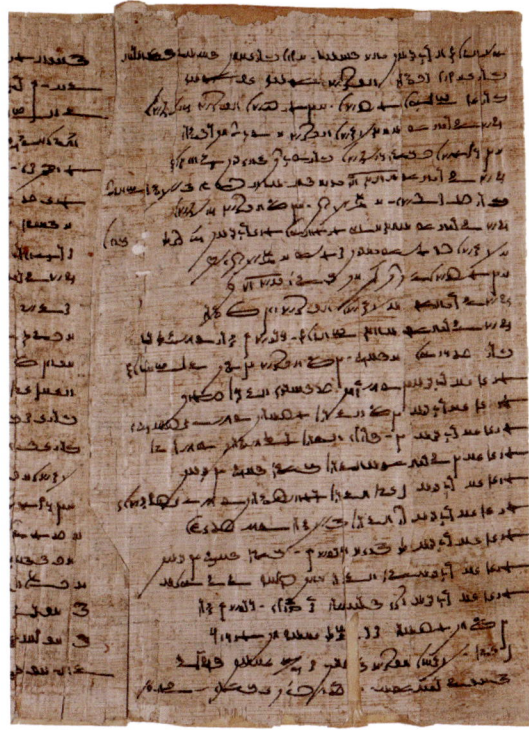

Fig. II.25. RMO inv.no. F 95/5.1, sheet 6: detail of column 12 of the Papyrus Insinger, Roman period (1st century AD), h. 26.7 cm.

all hopes of selling further antiquities to the RMO; however, the following years saw a complete shift in the existing constellation. Insinger's move to his self-built house in Luxor will have had the greatest impact on his own circumstances. At the same time, however, a number of other changes took place. Thus the year 1890 witnessed the transfer of the overcrowded Egyptian Museum in Cairo from the damp rooms in the disused custom's office on the waterfront at Bulaq to the former harîm palace of Ismail Pasha at Giza. One year after, Leemans finally left the directorship of the Leiden Museum, an event which was followed by his death in 1893; he was succeeded as director by Willem Pleyte. In 1892, the ineffectual Grébaut, who had made many enemies due to his inconsiderate and impetuous actions, was forced to resign from the position of director of the Antiquities Service. He was followed by the prehistorian Jacques de Morgan, who would be in office until 1897.[54]

Perhaps all these changes may explain the marked gap in the correspondence kept in the RMO archives. It rather looks as if the disappointed Insinger did not resume contact with the Leiden museum until 1894, when he again proposed to send more photographs. Pleyte hastened to stress that he would welcome renewed contact, adding that the Coptic textiles were now on display and that the publication on the Coptic manuscripts was almost ready.[55] This seems to have convinced Insinger that a new wind was blowing from Leiden, and accordingly his next letter of 18 November again mentions the possibility of purchasing objects for the museum, ideally by placing credits at his disposal. Pleyte was again quick in reacting, promising a budget of 100 to 150 Dutch guilders and specifying a wish list including ostraca, papyri, and pottery.[56] Early in January 1895, Insinger could confirm the purchase of more demotic ostraca, further announcing that he had started negotiations about the acquisition of two papyri from Akhmim.[57] More details were supplied a month later: the dealer was none other than the French consul Frénay whom we have met before with respect to the plunder of the Akhmim mummies; the papyrus (in two parts) had already been seen by Legrain[58] and was said to have a 'moral' subject; the price was stated as 4000 French francs; and Frénay was also negotiating with a French party.[59] What Insinger did not mention, was that in fact the papyrus had already been sent to the Louvre in Paris for inspection, where the curator Eugène Revillout could not resist partly unrolling it. In the process, he damaged the first eight columns of text, and then simply returned the violated manuscript to Akhmim because he considered the price too high.[60]

The following months showed what could be done in the acquisition of antiquities, provided that all parties concerned reacted in an efficient manner.[61] On February 21st, Pleyte asked the trustees of the museum for an extra acquisition budget of fl. 2.000 (the equivalent of the 4000 French francs), which was granted provisionally on March 14th. The next day he cabled to Insinger in Luxor 'please buy papyrus'. Another critical episode happened on April 9th, when another cable was received in Leiden, with the ominous words: 'expédiez argent ou papyrus perdu. Insinger'. The money was remitted by telegraph the same

---

54 Bierbrier 2012, 386; for Grébaut, see *ibid.*, 223. See also Thompson 2015, 64-71.
55 Appendix II, letter no. **15**, with Pleyte's answer in RMO Archives, dispatched letters, 1894/93.
56 Appendix II, letter no. **16**; Pleyte's answer in dispatched letters, 1894/285 (4 days later, so in fact the letters must have crossed each other).
57 Appendix II, letter no. **17**.
58 The French Egyptologist Georges Legrain (1865-1917) had been appointed as inspecteur-dessinateur of the Antiquities Service in 1894 and was mainly working at Amarna and Dahshur at the time. See Bierbrier 2012, 320-321.
59 Appendix II, letter no. **18**.
60 See Appendix II, letter no. **56**. For Charles Eugène Revillout (1843-1913), see Bierbrier 2012, 462-463. See also Appendix II, letter no. **47**, which mentions that Legrain photographed the missing beginning of the papyrus.
61 For the correspondence, see appendix I *sub* F 95/5.1.

Fig. II.26. RMO inv.no. F 95/8.9k: roll of linnen wrapping with fringed ends and blue and red end bands, from the mummy of Nesitanebasheru, 21st Dynasty, 510 x 12 cm.

day, and three days later Frénay confirmed he would send the papyrus to the Dutch consul-general in Cairo, Van der Does de Willebois. The latter protested that he could not take the manuscript, because he did not have the possibility to ship it to Europe by diplomatic courier (implying this was to be done without visitation?). In the end, an official export licence was received from De Morgan, and in May 1895 the papyrus arrived in Leiden via the Ministry of Foreign Affairs, and was registered by the museum under inventory number F 95/5.1 (Fig. II.25).

With the designation *Papyrus Insinger*, this beautiful demotic manuscript has become rightly famous as one of the last (and fullest) Egyptian books of wisdom. As such, it appears in most of the anthologies of Ancient Egyptian literature. Its earliest edition was entrusted to the able philologist Pieter Boeser, now the new curator of the RMO, who (together with Pleyte) published a lithographic reproduction in 1899, followed by a photo atlas in 1905, and finally by Boeser's transcription and German translation in 1920.[62] Upon unrolling in Leiden,[63] the full length of the papyrus (formerly estimated as 4.5 m by Frénay) was now established as 613 cm. Even so it soon proved to be incomplete, because both the beginning and the end of the manuscript were damaged and fragmentary. In the course of time, several of the missing fragments have turned up in collections in Cairo, Heidelberg, Paris, and Philadelphia, but nobody seems to have realised we have to blame Revillout for this unfortunate situation. It was common practice for 19th-century dealers to sell the fragments of a manuscript separately from the main text, so Frénay did not act in an unusual manner. Later, some other papyrus fragments with parallel texts in Copenhagen have demonstrated that the Leiden text was not unique but existed in several copies at the time. Even so, the Leiden version is by far the most complete. It seems to date from the 1st century AD, and it is very unfortunate that we shall probably never know its original provenance. Though 'Akhmim' is generally accepted, this is just based on the place of residence of the dealer Frénay, whereas it is well-known that dealers used to travel around, buying from local farmers and middlemen

---

62 Pleyte/Boeser 1899; Holwerda 1905; Boeser 1920. For a full bibliographical reference, see http://www.trismegistos.org/daht/detail.php?tm=55918.
63 This had been finished by the end of July: see RMO Archives, letters dispatched, 1895/199.

Fig. II.27. (above) RMO inv.no. F 99/1.432: ostracon with forged text, 8 x 14.5 cm.

Fig. II.28. (right) RMO inv.no. F 99/1.2: brick stamped with the name of Istemkheb, 21st Dynasty, 8 x 17 x 36.5 cm.

in various places. Even if we want to stick to Akhmim as provenance, it would be interesting to know the exact find-spot of the manuscript (an archive or private library in the ruins of the ancient town of Panopolis?), and its possible association with other objects.

The summer of 1895 was marked by Insinger's first-time visit to the Netherlands since the beginning of his self-imposed exile. After arriving at the house of his brother Willem (who had now moved to Bennekom), he was surprised to find there a shipment of royal mummy wrappings from Deir el-Bahari, sent over seven years previously and then destined for the museum.[64] These were now sent on to Leiden and registered there as inv.nos. F 95/8.6-13.[65] They proved to consist of samples of linen of various quality, with or without coloured bands, and cut from the mummies of Pinodjem II, Nesitanebasheru (Fig. II.26), Masaherta, Nesikhonsu, and others from the royal cachette at Deir el-Bahari, plus from an unknown mummy found in Sheikh Abd el-Qurna.[66] Clearly, these were some left-overs of the unwrappings of the royal mummies in 1886, when Insinger was allowed to wield his scissors. Another item included was a quantity of linseed from a Theban tomb (inv.no. F 95/8.5).

5. Potsherds and prehistory (1897-1901)

Early in 1895, Insinger announced that he was buying more ostraca, a message which was repeated from time to time until the actual arrival in Leiden of a crate with no less than 732 items in June 1897.[67] Insinger specified again that the bulk of these inscribed potsherds came from the ruins of Karnak, where villagers were sifting through the fertile debris (*sebakh*) and where he had now engaged a man to work for him. Pleyte specifically urged him to ask De Morgan's assistance for the transport to the Netherlands, and Insinger indeed contacted him, finding out

---

64 Appendix II, letter no. **27**.
65 Most numbers consist of several different samples; no. 11 is now lost.

66 For these textiles, see Van 't Hooft *et al.* 1994, cat.nos. 48, 50, 54-56, 66, 68-76, 78, 81-88, 197-207, 267-268.
67 Appendix II, letters nos. **17**, **22**, **29**, **31-34**.

Fig. II.29. RMO inv.no. F 1901/1.7: flint blade, neolithic period, l. 14 cm.

Fig. II.30. RMO inv.no. F 1901/1.21: slate palette, Nagada-I period, 12.3 x 55 cm.

Fig. II.31. RMO inv.no. F 1901/1.26: red-figured vessel, Nagada-II period, h. 14 cm.

Fig. II.32. RMO inv.no. F 1901/1.49: white-figured bowl, Nagada-Ic period, h. 7, diam. 18 cm.

he was already leaving his post as director of the Service.[68] In the end, the shipment was arranged by the Dutch consulate in Cairo via a consular agent and representative of the Rotterdam Lloyd in Port Said by the name of MacDonald. Upon arrival in Leiden the ostraca were registered as inv.nos. F 97/6.1-732.[69] By that time, Insinger was already buying more of this fascinating material, so that a new shipment arrived via the same route in January 1899 (inv.nos. F 99/1.5-484).[70] Again, the provenance was stated to be Karnak; other ostraca were available from Armant but Insinger did not manage to purchase these as yet. Some of the ostraca from the last shipment were in fact forgeries, as Insinger himself realised later (Fig. II.27).[71] Probably, this meant that the source where these documents came from was already drying up. The crate also contained a limestone inscription fragment (F 99/1.1) and three bricks stamped with the name of Istemkheb (inv.nos. F 99/1.2-4), said to be from 'Salamie' but in fact probably from Gebelein (Fig. II.28).[72]

Insinger first mentions the availability of objects found in Gebelein in a letter to Pleyte of 27 September 1896, though he then missed the opportunity to buy any.[73] This site, about 25 km south of Luxor on the west bank of the Nile, was first discovered in 1884. According to the normal custom of the time, Maspero ordered a foreman from Qurna to start excavations there on behalf of the Bulaq Museum, which was to receive half of the numerous finds. It was left to the excavator to do as he pleased with the other half.[74] Under the circumstances, it need not surprise us that nobody realised that Gebelein included one of the oldest cemeteries found so far, dating back to the neolithic period which was hardly known at the time. The objects arriving in Cairo were provision-

---

68 He was succeeded by Victor Loret (1859-1946), who was quite unsuited and had to leave in 1899; see Bierbrier 2012, 338-339.
69 For their publication, see again Nur el-Din 1974; Bagnall/Sijpesteijn/Worp 1980.
70 *Cf.* Appendix II, letters nos. **35-39**.
71 Appendix II, letters no. **41** and **50**.

72 Appendix II, letter no. **40**. El-Salmīya is a village close to Tod (see Porter/Moss 1937, 169 and map II), and Insinger may have bought the bricks there. He seems to imply they were found in a Roman well at that site, but this may have been a case of reuse of older building material. Their original provenance seems to be nearby Gebelein, see *ibid.* 164; Ritner 2009, 135.
73 Appendix II, letter no. **30**.
74 *Cf.* Maspero 1886, 80-83; Maspero 1887b, 208-210; Daressy 1922, 17, 26.

Fig. II.33. RMO inv.no. F 1901/1.45: Palace Ware jar, 18th Dynasty, h. 31, diam. 16 cm.

Fig. II.34. RMO inv.no. F 1901/1.62: terracotta offering table in the shape of a house model, Middle Kingdom, h. 27, w. 30, d. 47 cm.

ally classified as 'Dynasty XI' and it was not until much later that they attracted the attention of the specialists of Egyptian prehistory. By then, a large amount of the finds had already been dispersed in the art market, a practice which went on until after the turn of the century.[75] By 1910 the predynastic cemetery was said to be completely devoid of objects.[76]

In view of these developments, it is probable that the prehistoric pottery offered by Insinger in a letter of early 1899 was indeed from this provenance.[77] Pleyte expressed his interest, and accordingly Insinger started buying not only pots but also flint implements, palettes, and ivories. A first batch of these was sent to the consulate in Cairo by the end of August, but was left there by sheer negligence of the personnel ('those people do nothing!') and did not arrive in Leiden until January 1901. Altogether, there were 20 flint tools (Fig. II.29), 2 palettes (Fig. II.30), and 36 vessels of predynastic date (Figs. II.31-32). Otherwise the cargo included pottery vessels of pharaonic date (Fig. II.33), two terracotta offering tables likewise from Gebelein (Fig. II.34), 7 Graeco-Roman terracottas from Medinet Habu (Fig. II.35; another temple which was gradually being cleared of later debris)[78], several shabtis and glass vessels (Fig. II.36), plus almost 250 ostraca from Karnak and Armant. These objects were registered as inv. nos. F 1901/1.330, and they were followed by a second batch of three crates in August of the same year. These crates held 48 flint implements (Fig. II.37), 56 pots (Figs. II.38-39), and several palettes (Fig. II.40), amulets, mace-heads (Fig. II.41), and other prehistoric or Early Dynastic objects from Gebelein; another stamped brick and terracotta offering table (Fig. II.42) from the same provenance; several pottery vessels of New Kingdom or Coptic date; a number of figurines (including several blatant forgeries! Fig. II.43); and yet another set of 128 ostraca, especially from the area to the north of the quay of the Karnak temple (inv.nos. F 1901/9.1-293). Especially the predynastic material, which so far had been absent in Leiden and which was said to represent all the types distinguished by De Morgan,[79] formed a welcome addition to the museum collections.

---

75 *Cf.* Quibell 1901 for an object from Gebelein sold by a dealer in Qena.
76 Schiaparelli 1921, 127.
77 For the 1901 acquisitions, see Appendix II, letters nos. **40-47**, **49**. The quotation is from letter no. **43**.

78 See De Morgan 1896, 143-146.
79 Appendix II, letter no. **49**.

Fig. II.35. RMO inv.no. F 1901/1.74: terracotta figure of seated Harpokrates, Roman period, h. 18 cm.

Fig. II.36. RMO inv.no. F 1901/1.82: glass flask, Roman period, h. 15 cm.

Fig. II.37. RMO inv.no. F 1901/9.25: flint fishtail knife, neolithic period, 8.3 x 14.5 cm.

Fig. II.38. RMO inv.no. F 1901/9.69: black-topped jar, Nagada-II period, h. 36.5, diam. 16 cm.

Fig. II.39. RMO inv.no. F 1901/9.86: red-figured jar, Nagada-II period, h. 19.5, diam. 19 cm.

Fig. II.40. RMO inv.no. F 1901/9.58: tortoise-shaped palette, Nagada-II period, 7.9 x 8.0 cm.

Fig. II.41. RMO inv.no. F 1901/9.124-125: two mace-heads, Early Dynastic period, h. 3.0-6.7 cm.

Fig. II.42. RMO inv.no. F 1901/1.120: terracotta offering table in the shape of a house model, Middle Kingdom, h. 15.5, w. 36, d. 44 cm.

Though there is no explicit reference to export permits in the surviving correspondence, all crates duly passed via the Giza Museum for inspection and sealing.[80] With Insinger himself now living in Luxor, he just sent the crates to the Dutch consulate in Cairo, which took care of the paperwork at the Museum and the shipment to Europe. Under the lenient antiquities laws of the period, the cargo cannot have been very controversial and would have passed any visitation. The Antiquities Service had again come under the directorship of Insinger's old friend, the capable Gaston Maspero, who had returned from France for another turn of office (1899-1914).[81] The two gentlemen will not have met each other very regularly, but one such occasion may have been in October 1900, when Insinger was in Cairo for a doctor's visit.[82] Maspero's main worries during these years must have been the 1902 move of the Cairo Museum from its premises in Giza to the purpose-built museum building on Tahrir Square which it still inhabits.

Contacts with the RMO in Leiden also became less intensive, with curator Boeser sometimes answering Insinger's letters in the absence of Pleyte, who was on sick-leave. It may have been his failing health which made Pleyte less keen on the purchase of antiquities, and several offers to acquire coins, or more demotic and Coptic manuscripts,

Fig. II.43. (left) RMO inv.no. F 1901/1.118: forged terracotta figurine, h. 28 cm.

Fig. II.44. (above) RMO inv. no. F 1929/12.3: limestone stela of Parthenios, Roman period, h. 29.5, w. 18.5, d. 8 cm.

---

80 Appendix II, letters nos. **43**, **45**, **47**.
81 Bierbrier 2012, 360.
82 Appendix II, letter no. **47**.

Fig. II.45. (above) RMO inv. no. F 1929/12.10: funerary cone of Nebmehyt, 18th Dynasty, l. 19.5 cm.

Fig. II.46. (left) RMO inv.no. F 1929/12.28: Ptah-Sokar-Osiris statue, Ptolemaic period, h. 70 cm.

were dismissed. On 1 March 1903, Willem Pleyte died. He was succeeded as director of the RMO by the classical archaeologist A.E.J. Holwerda, who – together with his son, curator, and future successor J.H. Holwerda – focussed the museum's attention on the classical world and Dutch archaeology, rather than on the ancient oriental cultures. This explains that no further transactions were made with Insinger, and even the correspondence was soon dying down (though there was a faint revival in 1908-1909, when Insinger tried to sell more antiquities from Gebelein, gave some seals in loan,[83] and provided some news about additional parts of the Insinger Papyrus).[84]

6. Donations by descendants (1929-1957)

Insinger lived on for another fifteen years in his mansion at Luxor, and though he is said to have been an antiquities dealer, to the best of my knowledge so far none of his objects have surfaced in other collections. Some objects had been sent to his brother Willem's house in Bennekom during his lifetime, and others may have followed after his death, when *Palmenburg* was sold to the khedivial family. The brother was quick in asking

---

83   The seals are already mentioned in Appendix II, letters nos. **46**, **48**, and **55**.
84   Appendix II, letters nos. **53-56**.

Fig. II.47. RMO inv.no. F 1929/12.32: coffin for a falcon mummy, Graeco-Roman period, h. 48, w. 29, l. 55 cm.

Fig. II.48. RMO inv.no. F 1929/12.1: granodiorite statue of Osiris, Late period, h. 36.5 cm.

for the return of the seals and the photography collection loaned to the Leiden Museum.[85] It was not until 1929, when J.H. Holwerda (now museum director as his father's successor) was excavating a number of burial mounds on the Bennekom estate of the Insingers, that contact with the family was re-established. On that occasion, Insinger's sister-in-law C.A.S. Insinger-Everwijn Lange, the widow of his brother Willem, generously donated the remaining antiquities and some ethnographic objects to the museum.[86] There was a hand-written list of these objects, drawn up by Insinger himself, but this had to be returned to the family, so all we have is the list in the RMO inventory books which must have copied some of its information.

The objects were registered as nos. F 1929/12.1-78 and consisted of 3 stelae (Fig. II.44); a number of canopic jars, funerary cones (Fig. II.45), and shabtis; yet another terracotta house-shaped offering table, said to be from Thebes but probably from Gebelein like the others; 2 Ptah-Sokar-Osiris figures (Fig. II.46); and a number of smaller objects of various kinds. Among the more important ones was a beautiful rectangular coffin for a falcon-mummy (Fig. II.47) plus a number of fragments of others, all from Akhmim in view of good parallels with that provenance now in Cairo.[87] There was also a headless Osiris statue bought at Koptos, inscribed for an official Psamtekmen (Fig. II.48).[88] Of the 11 pots from various periods there were two from 'el-Mesjeich' (doubtless Nag' el-Mashayikh opposite Girga), one from Kurkur, and one found to the north of Aswan; all of these must have been found

---

85   RMO Archives, received letters, 29 August and 24 October 1919, 3 and 16 February 1920; dispatched letters, 3 September and 25 October 1919, 5 and 18 February 1920. This does not concern the photographic prints sent in 1888 (and which are still kept as property of the RMO) but merely the negatives temporarily deposited in Leiden in 1894 (the present whereabouts of which is unknown: according to the descendants of the Insinger family, there is nothing left of any archives).

86   RMO Archives, letters received from C.A.S. Insinger-Everwijn Lange, dated 5 December 1929, 10 September and 29 October 1930, and 14 July 1933; letters dispatched to her, dated 7 and 13 December 1929, 26 August and 23 October 1930. According to this information, the bulk of the material had been received from Egypt in 1890 in a crate badly broken during the transport; some objects could not be found at the time, and a large vase stayed behind in Bennekom.

87   The complete one has inv.no. F 1929/12.32 and is published in Van Wijngaarden 1931; Raven 1993, fig. 17. For the parallels in Cairo, see Gaillard/Daressy 1905, nos. 29796-29801. The JE number quoted there for CGC 29800 (26.099) means this object was acquired in 1884 (Bothmer 1974, 115).

88   Published by Van Wijngaarden 1933, 1-3 with fig. 1. This object occurs in Wilbour's notebook 2-F in Brooklyn: '27 Mar 83. Masp. bot of Sheikh Aly at Coptos: Basalt Os. frm shoulder to ankle: .38 of [follows hieroglyphic inscription]'. I wish to thank R.S. Bianchi for a copy of the relevant page. Sheikh Aly can be identified as Sheikh Ali Ledid; see Hagen/Ryholt 2016, 197.

Fig. II.49. RMO inv.no. F 1941/4.1: Corinthian amphora, Late period, h. 59 cm.

Fig. II.50. RMO inv.no. F 1956/10.1: mummy head of a woman, Roman period, h. 20.5 cm.

Fig. II.51. RMO inv.no. F 1956/10.3: mummy hand, New Kingdom (?), l. 20 cm.

Fig. II.52. RMO inv.no. F 1956/10.4: ibis mummy, Roman period, l. 40.5 cm.

Fig. II.53. (above) RMO inv.no. F 1956/10.7: package with serpent mummies, Roman period, l. 19.5 cm.

Fig. II.54. (right) RMO inv.no. F 1957/11.3: forged papyrus roll before unwrapping, l. c. 15 cm.

Fig. II.55. (above) RMO inv.no. F 1957/11.4: vessel, Late period, with fake seals and bandages, h. 11.5 cm.

Fig. II.56. (top) RMO inv.no. F 1984/1.38: tetradrachm of Diocletian, obverse, diam. 2.1 cm.

Fig. II.57. (bottom) RMO inv. no. F 1984/1.38: tetradrachm of Diocletian, reverse, diam. 2.1 cm.

during Insinger's exploits in Upper-Egypt together with Schelling in the year 1882. Even more important was a collection of 32 textiles from the royal cachette at Deir el-Bahari, allegedly taken from the mummies of Nesikhonsu, Nesitanebasheru, 'and others';[89] a collection of linseed, a lotus flower, and the fruit of an Indian lotus may be from the same provenance (though the latter has not been attested in Egypt before the Roman period).

The large vessel kept in Bennekom (footnote 86) was donated to the RMO after the death of Mrs Insinger-Everwijn Lange (inv.no. F 1941/4.1; Fig. II.49). It proves to be a Corinthian Type A amphora, and its provenance has been garbled as 'el-Kirchisch opposite Gizeh'.[90] But even that was not the last posthumous present received from Jan Herman Insinger. In 1956 his grandson Jan Herman Odo (a son of Edmond Herman Deodatus) contacted the museum about the presence of a number of Egyptian antiquities in a glass cabinet at the family house of Pijnenburg. These were inspected by Van Wijngaarden (then director of the RMO) and most of them were donated to the museum (inv. F 1956/10.1-7).[91] They consist of two heads and one hand of human mummies (Figs. II.50-51), three ibis mummies (Fig. II.52), and one package of serpent mummies (Fig. II.53).[92] Unfortunately, the original provenance of these mummies has not been recorded. A donation of a fake papyrus scroll (made up of assorted papyrus fragments and linen wrapped around a stick; Fig. II.54) and a small vessel, likewise with linen wrappings and provided with seals (Fig. II.55), was received in 1957 (inv. F 1957/11.3-4).[93]

A final present by Jan Herman Insinger's descendants was not registered until 1984 (F 1984/1.1-238). Yet the donation in question seems to have been received much earlier, *viz.* in 1929, from Mrs Insinger-Everwijn Lange. It concerns a collection of 238 Roman coins, ranging in time from Probus (276-282) to Galerius (305-311) and probably found in Luxor itself, where the Roman emperors had established an important *castra* inside the Luxor temple in the course of the 3rd century. The most conspicuous remains of this construction today are the paintings dated to the reign of Diocletian in some areas of the central temple, and indeed several of the coins bear his portrait (Figs. II.56-57). The coins may have been found during the removal of the many layers of later debris during the 1880s, or perhaps during further cleaning work by order of De Morgan in 1895.[94] The first time Insinger mentioned his coin collection was in a letter of July 1898, and he kept referring to the subject during the following two years.[95] Apparently part of them was already with his brother in Holland, and the whole collection was now offered for sale. Though Pleyte asked for further information, nothing came of it, and therefore the collection was still in Bennekom in 1929. Why it was not properly registered by the RMO at the time is puzzling: perhaps this was a matter of lack of expertise, or Van Wijngaarden may have considered donating the coins to the National Coin Collection. Thus the collection led a hidden existence in the museum's magazines until 1984.

---

89   Published by Van 't Hooft *et al.* 1994, cat.nos. 51-53, 60-65, 67, 77, 79, 91-110.
90   Possibly, this again refers to Nag' el-Mashayikh opposite Girga.
91   See RMO Archives, letters received from J.H.O. Insinger, dated 8 and 19 October 1956; letters dispatched by Van Wijngaarden, 17 and 24 October.
92   See Raven/Taconis 2005, cat.nos. 44-45, 54, 110-112, 127.
93   See RMO Archives, letters received from J.H.O. Insinger, dated 18 November 1957; letters dispatched by W.D. Van Wijngaarden, dated 14 and 22 November. The papyrus scroll has been dismantled for research and what is left of it is two glass frames full of papyrus fragments and a wooden stick with a clay sealing at either end. For such fakes, see Wilkinson 1858, 324-325: quoted in Hagen/Ryholt 2016, 148. The impressions on the pottery jar were applied with the same seal as that used on the papyrus stick, which is reason to believe they were also added by the same forger who made up the papyrus.
94   For the start of the excavations in January 1885, see Maspero 1886, 60. For De Morgan's activities, see Appendix II, letter no. **26**.
95   Appendix II, letters nos. **37-39, 41**.

Chapter III

Jan Herman Insinger and the antiquities trade of his time

1. Dealer or donator?

Jan Herman Insinger is often regarded as just another dealer in antiquities.[1] I hope the previous pages have shown that he was in fact much more than that: a passionate amateur-Egyptologist, a traveller and explorer, an able photographer, and a chronicler of the changing times he witnessed in Egypt. Besides, he was indeed a collectionneur who formed a habit of giving away or selling on parts of his private treasures, but did not mind hanging on to other objects till the end of his life. This is the picture that arises from his correspondence now kept in the archives of the Leiden Museum and elsewhere. It transpires from these letters that at least in the case of the RMO he cannot have made much profit from his transactions, and should rather be regarded as a benefactor of the museum.

Thus, the objects received in 1882 were donations by Schelling and Insinger, and there were no charges for the transport either. Schelling was carrying a budget for acquisitions from the National Museum of Ethnography, and the RMO objects were partly packed with those destined for the other Leiden museum. The objects acquired in 1886 were registered by the museum as purchases, but Insinger just asked to be remunerated for his own costs, including the transport, and was not making any profit for himself if we may believe his letters. The costs for the Coptic manuscripts were stated to be £ 12 (or in Dutch guilders: fl. 120) for about 150 sheets, and in the end the museum paid fl. 122.[2] This was said to be very cheap, since the Bibliothèque Nationale already paid 2-3 guilders per sheet, and the British Museum about 8 guilders.[3] The two mummies from Akhmim and their coffins were charged at £ 8 by Maspero,[4] and the museum paid no more than fl. 97 for the whole set.[5] Insinger did not wish to charge for the packing and transport either, because the museum was on such a tight budget. We know that in 1894 a mummy and coffin could be bought at the sale's room of the Cairo Museum for £20-30,[6] so this transaction can be considered as a very good bargain. The ostraca and

---

1 *Cf.* Hagen/Ryholt 2016, 224-225. However, see Thompson 2015, 124-125, who quotes a letter of Percy Newberry to Warren R. Dawson, dated 15 February 1949 (ibid. 215 n. 42): 'I should not describe him as a dealer in antiquities'.
2 Archives RMO, 18.1/6: Accounts 1885-1888, payment to W.A. Insinger on 2 June 1886.
3 Appendix II, letter no. **6**. We generally reckon with an exchange rate of £ 1 (the Egyptian pound was considered to be more or less equal in value to the British pound) = about fl. 10 to 12,50 (Dutch guilders) = fr. 20 (French francs).
4 Appendix II, letters nos. **6-7**, **9**.
5 Archives RMO, 18.1/6: Accounts 1885-1888, payment to W.A. Insinger on 5 March 1887.
6 Hagen/Ryholt 2016, 47-48.

textiles acquired in 1888 were paid at fl. 40,[7] no more than the costs of transport only.[8] If we reckon that in 1930 one ostracon cost 5 piasters (the equivalent of fl. 0,50),[9] this was a good price for 132 ostraca plus the textiles and complete pots.

It was a different matter with the Papyrus Insinger, purchased from Frénay in 1895. Here the museum had to pay the amount of fl. 2000, the equivalent of the 4000 French francs asked by Frénay, which could only be paid thanks to an occasional raise in the museum's budget granted by the Ministry.[10] This was an exceptional price paid for an exceptional papyrus of over 6 metres long. If we compare this with the amount of £ 200 (*i.e.* about fl. 2,000) paid for a single sheet of hieratic in 1930,[11] it cannot have been too expensive. Unless Insinger shared the profit with Frénay – for which there is no evidence – he does not seem to have made any money on the transaction himself.

No bill was found for the transport of the forgotten antiquities in 1895. The 732 ostraca received in 1897 were charged at fl. 18, and in the end the museum paid Insinger a sum of fl. 19,95.[12] The 481 ostraca and 3 bricks purchased in 1899 cost fl. 15,88.[13] The two shipments of 1901, over 600 objects altogether, cost fl. 123,13 and fl. 177, respectively.[14] This amounts to an average price per object of about 6 Dutch cents, or less than an Egyptian piaster. Clearly, Insinger was not making any money on these transactions.

It may have been different with his other commercial activities. We have seen that among the Dutch diplomats in Cairo, he had a reputation of being an unscrupulous usurer. This may have been his behaviour towards the indigenous population, for whom he is said to have served as a money-lender. On the whole Insinger cannot be blamed for marked colonial or racist feelings, and in fact the much more narrow-minded Wilbour was rather shocked to notice how freely Insinger's children were allowed to play with the little son of his boat's captain.[15] Insinger's anti-British feelings also gave him a certain solidarity with the cause of the native Egyptians. However, the local farmers were going through a difficult period during the first decennia of British rule, with the ensuing changes in agricultural policy, taxing, and irrigation, and perhaps Insinger had to be strict with them in order to get his money back. It was common practice to ask for antiquities as a security for such loans of money,[16] and in this way Insinger may have acquired many objects picked up by the farmers while looking for fertile earth (*sebakh*) in the ancient ruins, or while conducting illegal excavations. In this manner, Insinger may have acted as an intermediary between the locals and the tourists, who seem to have come to his house for buying ancient souvenirs. Still, we do not know anything about the extent of this commerce, and as said before, no objects sold by him to other parties than the RMO have become known to us so far.

2. Abiding by the law

Another aspect of Insinger's activities as an art dealer that we need to consider here is of course the question whether he was operating within the boundaries set by contemporary law. From a modern point of view,[17] it is astounding to see how easily a foreigner like Insinger could get involved in the commerce of antiquities, in their export to Europe, and even in the exploitation of hitherto unknown cemeteries, monasteries, temples, or domestic sites. Still, we have already stressed above that in most cases there is explicit evidence that he asked the authorities representing the Egyptian Antiquities Service for permission to ship objects to the Netherlands. This could be verified for the shipments of 1882 (pottery and stelae)[18] and 1886 (Coptic manuscripts and mummies from Akhmim).[19] The ostraca and textiles sent in 1888 clearly belonged to a class of objects that was not highly valued at the time, and the samples of linen from the royal cache of the same shipment were cut under Maspero's very eyes and obviously with his permission.

The Papyrus Insinger in 1895 was another matter. The Dutch consul-general in Cairo, who received this precious object, protested that he had no *valise diploma-*

---

7   Archives RMO, letters dispatched, 1888/67; see also 18.1/6: Accounts 1885-1888, payment to W.A. Insinger on 6 April 1888.
8   Appendix II, letter no. **10**.
9   Hagen/Ryholt 2016, 172. However, Insinger himself mentions 3 to 8 ostraca for 1 piaster (or 12½ cent): Appendix II, letters nos. **22** and **29**.
10 Including packing, transport, and the costs of the telegraphic payment the costs amounted to fl. 2,235. See Archives RMO, 18.1/9: Accounts 1895-1897, declaration of 19 September 1895.
11 *Cf.* Hagen/Ryholt 2016, 173.
12 Appendix II, letter no. **32**; Archives RMO, 18.1/9: Accounts 1895-1897, declaration of 27 June 1897. The costs of transport were another fl. 8,70.
13 Archives RMO, 18.1/10: Accounts 1898-1900, declaration of 21 March 1900 (plus an additional fl. 16,13 paid for transport on 3 February 1899).
14 Archives RMO, 18.1/10: Accounts 1898-1900, declaration of 12 January 1901; 18.1/11: Accounts 1901-1903, declaration of 29 August 1901. The transport cost fl. 30,43 and fl. 66,64, respectively.

15 Capart 1936, 534.
16 Hagen/Ryholt 2016, 125.
17 According to the Egyptian Law on the Protection of Antiquities of 6 August 1983 (also known as Law no. 117), all antiquities are regarded as the property of the state and the commerce in and export of antiquities is strictly forbidden.
18 Appendix II, letters nos. **1-2**, which at least imply some of the objects were shown to Maspero.
19 Appendix II, letters nos. **4** (some manuscripts seen by Maspero) and **6** (both mummies bought from Maspero).

tique and that the shipment would therefore be inspected like that of every private person.[20] However, it was soon obvious that the export of such an important piece had to be cleared with De Morgan (then head of the Antiquities Service), and the latter readily gave his official permission.[21] The later transports of 1897, 1899, and 1901 concerned ostraca, pottery, and other small objects: not the kind of material that would interest the Antiquities Service. Insinger even mentions that De Morgan was very helpful in allowing the export of antiquities to foreign museums, with the exception of first-class objects,[22] and that he personally assisted in organising the transport of the first crate with ostraca.[23] The following transports were likewise officially approved and sealed at the Giza Museum, then sent in the same manner by the Cairo consulate via Port Said harbour.[24]

The picture that transpires from these proceedings is consistent with the other information at our disposal and with the common practice at the time.[25] The first legislation trying to curb the uncontrolled loss of cultural heritage in Egypt was passed in 1835, when the export of antiquities was forbidden and the establishment of a museum for those objects already in the possession of the state or seized by the customs authorities was announced.[26] This museum was indeed installed in a small building in Ezbekiya Gardens in Cairo, and later transferred to the Citadel. However, this establishment was later abolished again, and the ban on export was only valid for objects of special importance and for persons who had not provided themselves with a special licence. In practice, this did not stop the widespread loot of antiquities continuing as before. It was not until 1858 that the French archaeologist Auguste Mariette founded the Egyptian Museum (Fig. III.1) and the *Service des Antiquités de l'Égypte*, serving as first director of both institutions until his death in 1881.[27] In theory, he was the only authority who could organise excavations all over Egypt, and indeed he was active on about thirty different sites, often more or less simultaneously. In practice, the demand to develop the young science of Egyptology convinced him of the necessity to grant excavation permits to foreign archaeological missions, who were then entitled to a proportion of their

Fig. III.1. Interior of the Cairo Museum with freshly arrived coffin from the tomb of Sennedjem. Photo by J.H. Insinger, 17.2 x 12.2 cm, Archives RMO.

finds (usually about half), the other part remaining in the possession of the state.[28]

But the Antiquities Service could also licence private individuals, such as local foremen attached to their excavations, native dealers of antiquities, and even notorious families of tomb robbers. This was the system used to cope with the sudden discoveries of provincial cemeteries or other archaeological remains thought to be of minor value, such as the above-mentioned necropoleis of Akhmim (where a gang of local entrepreneurs was headed by the French mill-owner Frénay) and Gebelein (where a *sheikh* Omar from Qurna was allowed to do as he pleased). Officially, such persons were working on behalf of the government, and half of their finds were destined for the Cairo Museum,[29] but for lack of proper supervision they may have pocketed much more than the other half granted to them, and which they could then sell to others. Frénay

---

20 Appendix II, letter no. **24**.
21 Archives RMO, letters received 1895/110 from the Ministry of the Interior; letters dispatched 1895/146 of Pleyte to De Morgan.
22 Appendix II, letter no. **30**.
23 Appendix II, letter no. **31**.
24 Appendix II, letters nos. **43, 45, 47**.
25 For the following, see Khater 1960; Hagen/Ryholt 2016, 133-146.
26 Khater 1960, 37-42.
27 Bierbrier 2012, 355-357. *Cf.* Khater 1960, 3-4. For a recent discussion of the episode, see Reid 2002, 99-107. Mariette's policy was continued more or less unchanged by his immediate successors.

28 *Cf.* Hagen/Ryholt 2016, 119. This system was still in common use in the first half of the 20th century: see Erman 1929, 215. It was stopped to be a fixed right by a new law of 1951, and in fact already in 1923 (Khater 1960, 165-173).
29 See Appendix II, letter no. **5**.

Fig. III.2. Luxor as it was: south end of the temple with the French house on top. Photo by J.H. Insinger, 12.1 x 16.5 cm, Archives RMO.

was an especially problematic person, since he acquired the authority of French consul, and therefore enjoyed a diplomatic immunity which he could even extend over the people working for him.[30]

Of course, the authorities were aware of the fact that the majority of finds was not made during licenced excavations but during illegal ones by unauthorized parties, or as a result of agricultural or construction work, the digging for *sebakh* or for irrigation projects, and other activities. The problem was that objects found on private land rightfully belonged to the owner of the land (as confirmed again by a High Order issued by Ismail Pasha in 1869),[31] and therefore a lively trade in antiquities sprang up to cater for the tourists, the private collectors, and the representatives of foreign museums. It was rare for these parties to buy straight from *fellahin* or other villagers, and in most cases they would go to middlemen and small dealers, or even to the first-class dealers who could afford a proper shop in one of the tourist places such as Cairo or Luxor.[32] It was not until 1912 that a new law became active, expecting the dealers to register with the Antiquities Service, which would then give them an official numbered licence.[33] From then onwards, all persons leaving the country with antiquities were likewise expected to report these to the authorities at the Cairo Museum, and were liable to be visited by the customs officials unless they could show a written export permit.[34]

---

30 Hagen/Ryholt 2016, 32-37 (with Frénay mentioned on page 35), 134.
31 Hagen/Ryholt 2016, 138.
32 For the various kinds of dealers, see Hagen/Ryholt 2016, 29-45.
33 Hagen/Ryholt 2016, 137-139; see also their Appendix 1 for the full text of this law.
34 Hagen/Ryholt 2016, 134-135.

Among the dealers, again, a special category was formed by the consuls of the various nations (Fig. III.2), and because of the immunity involved it was a very lucrative prospect if they managed to acquire this diplomatic status. It meant that their premises could not be raided and inspected by the authorities, as was done for instance in 1888 by the controversial new director of the Service, Eugène Grébaut, and that they could forward antiquities under the diplomatic seal.[35] It has occasionally been stated that Insinger himself had the position of a local consul in Luxor, referring to the Dutch flag that he used to fly from the tower of Palmenburg. However, I have found no proof of such a status in the consular records in the National Archives at The Hague. On the contrary, we have noticed above how unpopular Insinger was with the consular staff in Cairo, and that he frequently complained about their total lack of cooperation in the transport of antiquities to the Netherlands. It is true that in his letters he keeps recurring to the desirability of appointing a Dutch consular agent in Luxor, because such a person could do so much more in the field of acquiring antiquities for the Leiden Museum.[36] At the same time, he says explicitly that he did not have his own person in mind, but rather one of the local dealers in antiquities, a most reliable man whom he happened to know.

Though this person's name is never mentioned, there is no doubt that he was talking about Mohammed Mohassib Bey (1843-1928), because Wilbour also states that this dealer was very close with Insinger.[37] He also had the reputation of being the most reliable and influential dealer in Luxor.[38] Insinger's exertions have later been understood as an offer of immunity to Mohassib under the Dutch flag,[39] but it was of course the other way round: Insinger's Dutch flag (and his excellent contacts with the direction of the Antiquities Service) only provided symbolic immunity, but if Mohassib could acquire consular status, that would provide a much more effective protection and be to their mutual interest. In spite of the fact that Van der Does de Willebois (the Dutch consul-general in Cairo) declared that he did not object to such an appointment, he expected the Foreign Secretary in The Hague to set the first steps.[40] Accordingly, Leemans wrote to the Ministry with a proper request, but this was refused.[41] Some correspondence between Van der Does and the Home Secretary, Jan Heemskerk, now kept in the National Archives in The Hague, proves that this matter was in fact more complicated.[42] Van der Does argued that the task foreseen for Mohassib (who is here mentioned by name, thus confirming our identification of the nominee) would not be in accordance with Egyptian law, and the Egyptian government would only grant the status of Dutch consul to one of the inhabitants of Luxor already serving as diplomatic agent for one of the other nationalities. He added that personally he would object to the nomination of a native in view of the risk of corruption involved. Under the circumstances, Heemskerk had to dismiss the request.

As a result of this verdict, Insinger could only continue operating in his usual manner. With the failed prospect of diplomatic immunity for his activities and the lack of cooperation of the consulate in Cairo, he had no choice but to carry on in a careful way, relying instead on his good relationship with the representatives of the Antiquities Service and the Cairo Museum. In the end, this has served him very well, because people like Maspero and De Morgan, and even the difficult Grébaut, seem to have liked him and were quite willing to allow the export of objects that they could only regard as being second-rank and having no importance for the national collections. The fact that these objects were going to enrich another museum is repeatedly mentioned as another decisive factor. Unlike the curator of the British Museum, Wallis Budge, who was quite notorious for his illicit activities and was always trying to outwit the despised French colleagues of the Service,[43] Insinger never fell in disgrace and always behaved in an honest manner.

Above, I have already referred to a conflict between Insinger and Budge in 1903. It may well be that the former blamed the latter for his unethical behaviour because he saw Budge as a terrible competitor in the acquisition of antiquities, who was spoiling the market with the excessive prices he was prepared to pay and with the support he enjoyed from the side of the British colonial administration.[44] Still, the wording of his letter to *Le Phare d'Alexandrie* rather rings of an authentic moral conviction: he complains of 'the clandestine dispatch to Europe of antiquities taken surreptitiously from poorly guarded

---

35 Wilson 1964, 86-88; Hagen/Ryholt 2016, 35. For Grébaut's fight with antiquities dealers, see Thompson 2015, 26-28.
36 Appendix II, letters nos. **5**, **7**, **13**, **29**.
37 Capart 1936, 463, 494.
38 Hagen/Ryholt 2016, 245.
39 Wilson 1964, 102. For Mohassib, see Wilson 1964, 226; Hagen/Ryholt 2016, 245-247. Mohassib was the most prominent art dealer of Luxor, apart from being a land-owner and a very rich person.
40 Appendix II, letter no. **7**.
41 Archives RMO, letters dispatched 1888/197 of 17 November; letters received 1887/31 of 18 February.
42 National Archives, The Hague, file no. 2.05.38/1497: letter of Van der Does de Willebois to Home Secretary Heemskerk of 7 January 1887; letter of Heemskerk to Van der Does of 18 February 1887.
43 For Ernest Alfred Thompson Wallis Budge (1857-1934), see Bierbrier 2012, 90-92; Ismail 2011; Thompson 2015, 167-170. For some of his most notorious exploits, see Wilson 1964, 86-92, 130; James 1981, 23-25. See also Hagen/Ryholt 2016, 135-136.
44 *Cf.* Appendix II, letter no. **51** ('that man Budge').

excavations, sanctioning the plundering of the royal tombs, defrauding Egypt, to the advantage of "the most favoured nation", of ancestral documents, those whose rightful ownership can the least be disputed.'[45] These words sound surprisingly modern, and can be compared to those used in present-day conventions by UNESCO and other parties.[46] Few of his contemporaries would have felt as strongly about a nation's rightful ownership of its cultural heritage, and in this respect Insinger was certainly ahead of his time. The fact that he had lived in the country for almost twenty-five years when he wrote these lines may have helped him in identifying with the perspective of the native Egyptians, something few Europeans could imagine. Insinger's ethical motives also seem to transpire from his letter about the illegal deal offered by Emil Brugsch with respect to the textile samples in 1884,[47] and it probably came as a relief to hear that Leemans found an excuse not to proceed with the matter. The result of this moral attitude is that Insinger could preserve a clean conscience about his commercial activities in the years 1882-1901, and – unlike many other museums of antiquities dealing with Egypt in the same years – so can the RMO nowadays.

3. Missed opportunities

Of course, there is another side to this matter: if the Foreign Ministry and the Home Secretary of the Netherlands, the diplomatic staff in Cairo, and the successive directors of the Leiden Museum would have been a little more enterprising, so much more could have been perpetrated in the period under consideration. For the purpose of acquiring important collections of Egyptian art, the years 1880-1912 (before the new antiquities law was enacted) counted once again as a golden era – second only to the initial gold-rush of the early years of the century, immediately following Napoleon's Egyptian campaign. The difference with the earlier period was the presence of an Antiquities Service which tried to control the export of Egypt's cultural heritage. However, it can hardly be said that the organisation was very successful, or very strict for that matter.

As a tribute to the founder of the Service, Auguste Mariette, all his successors were French by tradition, and of course this meant that they took the interests of the European museums (and especially the Louvre) into account. Maspero had been head of the newly founded *École française du Caire* (which was to become the *Institut français d'Archéologie Orientale*) before he was appointed as Mariette's successor in 1881. Inevitably, this made him especially lenient towards French excavators, who were favoured by very generous *partages* at the end of their field campaigns.[48] With the increase of British political power in Egypt, following the events of 1882, the directors of the Service had to strike a new balance in order to preserve their position. The foundation of the *Egypt Exploration Fund* in 1882 brought a new player into the field,[49] and controversies over the allotment of excavation sites, the division of finds, or the export of antiquities were bound to be considered in the light of mounting British-French rivalry. British archaeologists rightly blamed the Service for its inefficiency, and the reputation of Maspero's notorious assistant Emil Brugsch was another source of criticism. Under the circumstances, it is not surprising that Maspero turned a blind eye to some of the practices of Wallis Budge, especially when young British inspectors of antiquities such as Howard Carter started to obtain positions in the Service. Thus a whole number of exports were allowed which were in fact quite illegal by contemporary standards.

More European countries followed the example of the French and the British and used the opportunity to enrich their national museums of antiquities by starting large-scale excavations in Egypt. Thus the year 1898 brought the advent of the Deutsche Orient Gesellschaft, in 1899 Reisner started his fieldwork for the joined mission of Harvard University and the Boston Museum of Fine Arts, and from 1903 also the Italians under Ernesto Schiaparelli undertook various projects in the field. Insinger explicitly suggested the possibility to start a separate Dutch campaign in one his letters,[50] but nothing came of it and the first Dutch archaeological mission was only started by Adolf Klasens at Abu Roash in 1957.[51] By then, the best period for acquiring objects as part of a *partage* was already over, though the RMO can certainly not complain about the generosity of the Egyptian colleagues with regard to the excavations at Abu Roash or later in Nubia.

Of course, excavations were not the only means of acquiring a collection, and the activities of Budge showed how much an energetic museum curator could do in this respect, by travelling to Egypt almost on a yearly basis and establishing personal contact with the leading dealers of antiquities. None of the Leiden Egyptologists ever visited

---

45 As translated by James 1992, 77.
46 For the text of the 1970 UNESCO Convention, see http://portal.unesco.org/en/ev.php-URL_ID=13039&URL_DO=DO_TOPIC&URL_SECTION=201.html (accessed on 1 November 2016).
47 Appendix II, letter no. **3**.

48 For a good impression of the treasures allotted to the Louvre in these years, see Desroches-Noblecourt/Vercoutter 1981. The manner in which Maspero allowed the bulk of the Akhmim Coptic manuscripts to be acquired for the Bibliothèque Nationale is another example of this partiality.
49 For the successes of British fieldwork, see James 1982.
50 Appendix II, letter no. **54**.
51 For the history of Dutch excavations in Egypt, see Raven 2007.

Egypt before the Nile trip made by Boeser in 1903.[52] Yet Insinger frequently urged Pleyte to visit him in Luxor and see the country with his own eyes.[53] Other possibilities mentioned were the appointment of a special agent for the purpose of acquisitions (a capacity which Schweinfurth was said to fulfil for the Berlin Museum)[54] or the foundation of a society for the same end.[55] Nothing was done with these suggestions. We have already discussed Insinger's fruitless endeavours to realise the appointment of a Dutch consul in Luxor.

Another of Insinger's suggestions, to place at his disposal an advance credit for purchases so that he did not have to await permission from Leiden before striking a deal, was only realised in 1895 when it was fixed at fl. 100-150, later raised to fl. 500 in 1900,[56] small sums when compared with the contemporary acquisitions by the British Museum[57] or (later) the Metropolitan Museum of Art.[58] Whereas other museums and even private individuals were buying sculptures, reliefs, and gold jewellery, Leemans and Pleyte seem to have felt that the Leiden Museum did not need any additions of that kind, asking Insinger to look out for ostraca, pottery, and other small finds instead.[59] The argument was that acquisition funds were lacking, yet when during all those years they made a single request for an occasional budget (*scil.* for the Papyrus Insinger), this was immediately granted by the Ministry. At the same time, the RMO was spending considerable amounts on objects from other ancient cultures. By way of example, we may take the same year 1895 when the Papyrus Insinger was bought: according to the account books more than fl. 4,250 was spent on the acquisition of Greek terracottas, vases, and marble sculptures; Roman glass, pottery, and coins; Roman and medieval metal objects; and even Indian antiquities in that single year.[60] Thus, the museum was clearly not lacking in money, but somehow the sense of urgency was missing in the acquisition policy. Of course, the RMO had been one of the foremost Egyptian collections in the world ever since 1830, but so were the British Museum and the Louvre which were nonetheless frantically expanding their collections during the same years 1879-1918 when Insinger was active in Egypt.

Insinger's letters give a clear impression of the lost opportunities of these years. In 1886 he already informed Leemans that the Cairo Museum was selling duplicates and other superfluous material from recent excavations.[61] Later that year he explicitly mentioned the possibility of acquiring shabtis (150 different types were said to be available), including the beautiful blue-glazed specimens from Deir el-Bahari,[62] but Leemans did not react. Clearly, Insinger was referring to shabtis from the royal cache, which had been found in 1881. Some of these attractive figurines, inscribed for Pinodjem I, Istemkheb, Maatkare and Nesikhonsu were bought by the RMO between 1931 and 1973, and they cost a great deal more than the 10 French francs per piece asked by Maspero.[63]

After the appointment of Grébaut as the new director of the Service, Insinger again sent a report to Leiden, mentioning the possibility to purchase Old Kingdom statues and stelae from the overcrowded Bulaq Museum.[64] At first Leemans showed his interest, asking to be sent a list of what was available, but later he asserted that Old Kingdom art was not so rare in the Leiden Museum as assumed.[65] This was manifestly incorrect at the time,[66] and even nowadays the Old Kingdom is not a very strong aspect of the RMO collections. Nothing came of this offer, which seems to have concerned monuments from Mariette's excavations at Saqqara. Because of the present-day focus on Saqqara in the RMO fieldwork in Egypt, it can only be deplored that this splendid opportunity was not put to a good use.

In 1888, Insinger repeated that Grébaut would be eager to sell duplicates to museums (rather than to private collectors),[67] and again Leemans asked for a detailed list but did not otherwise show any initiative.[68] Insinger gave up on the inert director and only resumed his endeavours after the appointment of his old friend Pleyte. In spite of the fact that the latter sent him a wish-list and

---

52 Van Wijngaarden 1935, 16.
53 Appendix II, letters nos. **29-30**, **35**, **49**, **51**.
54 Appendix II, letter no. **13**. For Leemans's negative reaction, see Archives RMO, letters dispatched, 1886/128. For Georg August Schweinfurth (1836-1925), see Bierbrier 2012, 497.
55 Appendix II, letter no. **30**.
56 Archives RMO, letters dispatched, 1894/285, 1898/98, and 1900/91.
57 For Budge as a big spender, see Hagen/Ryholt 2016, 116, 142 (no less than 74 boxes on one occasion!), 246 (£ 1500 for a granite statue).
58 *Cf.* Hagen/Ryholt 2016, 246 for the Metropolitan Museum spending £ 53,000 on the purchase of a set of jewellery – about a thousand times the budget which the RMO placed at Insinger's disposal!
59 Archives RMO, letters dispatched, 1894/285, 1900/91, and 1901/190.
60 Archives RMO, 18.1/9: Accounts 1895-1897.

61 Appendix II, letter no. **5**.
62 Appendix II, letter no. **6**.
63 *Cf.* Schneider 1977, cat. nos. 4.3.0.1, 4.3.0.3-6 (not, however, no. 4.3.0.8 because this belongs to Henttawy D who was not buried in the royal cache; see Kitchen 1973, 56-57).
64 Appendix II, letter no. **8**.
65 Archives RMO, letters dispatched, 1886/177 and 182.
66 A good impression of the Old Kingdom holdings of the collection in this period (but after the 1904 acquisition of a mastaba chapel) is given by Holwerda/Boeser/Holwerda 1905: little more than 3 statues, 1 relief, 1 offering table, and 1 sarcophagus. More reliefs and architectural elements were acquired after this publication was issued.
67 Appendix II, letter no. **14**.
68 Archives RMO, letters dispatched, 1888/220.

Fig. III.3. Insinger's house at Luxor, Palmenburg. Reproduction in the archives of the RMO.

an open credit, and that the more efficient cooperation worked very well in the case of the acquisition of the Papyrus Insinger, more precious opportunities were missed in the following years. Thus in 1895 Insinger mentioned the possibility of acquiring some demotic contracts,[69] and in 1896 he reported that Grébaut's successor De Morgan would be willing to assist in the export of antiquities to foreign museums.[70] In 1898 he offered to buy objects from the new royal tombs found by Loret in the Valley of the Kings, stating that many finds were being dispersed via the art market.[71] In 1901, he proposed to purchase some demotic papyri and Coptic manuscripts on parchment.[72] After Pleyte's death, Insinger established contact with Boeser, offering to buy more antiquities from Gebelein while the exploitation of the cemeteries was going on.[73] None of these opportunities was followed up.

4. Conclusions

Insinger was without any doubt the RMO's most important purveyor of Egyptian antiquities in the period 1879-1918, the years of his prolonged stay in Egypt. Altogether, he provided about 2,500 objects of various kinds. Among them were important categories of aegyptiaca hitherto missing from the Leiden collections or represented by a few stray items only. This especially concerns the categories of Coptic manuscripts,[74] Coptic and pharaonic textiles,[75] prehistoric material, and ostraca, and to a lesser extent also Coptic pottery and Roman coins. Very important is also that Insinger gave information on the provenance of this material, although of course by our modern standards this seriously

---

69 Appendix II, letter no. **24**.
70 Appendix II, letter no. **30**.
71 Appendix II, letter no. **35**. For a convenient list of Loret's work, see Reeves/Wilkinson 1996, 68-69. For the problem of objects being stolen by the workmen of excavations, see Hagen/Ryholt 2016, 91, 103.
72 Appendix II, letter no. **49**.
73 Appendix II, letter no. **54**.
74 Pleyte/Boeser 1897, 441-486 mentions the presence of no more than 5 small papyri and 1 codex, prior to the arrival of the Akhmim manuscripts.
75 According to Van 't Hooft *et al.* 1994, 6-7, 193, the collection comprised no Coptic textiles before the acquisitions made by Insinger.

Fig. III.4. Insinger and his eldest daughter Mina on board his dahabiya. Reproduction in the archives of the RMO.

lacks in detail. Still, when compared with the earlier collections acquired at the beginning of the 19th century and which arrived with hardly any indication of provenance, this was already a great step forward. Insinger's most important acquisition was of course the wisdom papyrus which has deservedly been named after him: the Papyrus Insinger features in all the anthologies of Ancient Egyptian literature and is justly famous as the last product of its genre of wisdom texts.[76] Most Egyptologists only know Jan Herman Insinger from this single document. I hope the present survey has demonstrated that in fact there is a lot more which we owe to this fascinating person.

Moreover, the research presented above has also enabled us to redress a number of unfounded verdicts pronounced with regard to Insinger's activities in Egypt. In the first place, there is the often repeated statement that Insinger used his consular immunity as a cover-up for his commercial activities.[77] We have found no proof that Insinger ever held a diplomatic position; on the contrary, his endeavours to get Mohammed Mohassib appointed as Dutch consul and his animosity vis-à-vis the Cairo consulate clearly imply that he did not have diplomatic status himself, as does the lack of pertinent documents in the consular archives in The Hague.

Secondly, rumour sometimes has it that Insinger was involved in illegitimate activities.[78] However, the survey of his activities clearly indicates that he was a personal friend of most representatives of the Antiquities Service, that he used to contact them about his purchases, and that they assisted him in exporting his treasures to the Netherlands. In

---

76 Von Bissing 1955, 91-120; Bresciani 1969, 585-610; Lichtheim 1980, 184-217; Brunner 1988, 295-349.
77 *Cf.* Wilson 1964, 102-103.
78 This seems to be implied by the reference to his 'peculiar position' in Luxor in the quotation from *The Egyptian Gazette* in Budge 1920, 367; James 1992, 78.

fact, our records suggest that Insinger was much more scrupulous than most of his contemporaries, and one of the few people to observe the law, or to realise that the Egyptian people had the right to preserve its cultural heritage.

Thirdly, most of the secondary sources assert that Insinger was a professional dealer in antiquities.[79] However, our archival material has shown that in fact he did not make a profit on the objects sold to the Leiden Museum, asking merely for compensation of the costs made in acquisition and transport. Moreover, some of these objects were clearly donations, whereas no evidence has been found to prove that he was also selling to other parties.[80]

Fourth, especially Wilson has sketched a completely false image of Insinger as a thin-pursed man, eking out his life in running errands for people like Wilbour.[81] It is a pity that Insinger has not been able to receive Wilson in his grand mansion of Palmenburg (Fig. III.3), which even impressed Wilbour (who was a millionaire himself). Clearly, Insinger could do more or less as he pleased, thanks to the financial backing of his affluent family in Holland and with the income from his land-leases, his money-lending, and perhaps even his occasional sale of antiquities. Probably, collecting was a pastime and personal hobby, rather than the basis for a profitable business.

Fifth, it has been asserted that Insinger was a resident in Luxor from 1879 onwards.[82] This is belied by various documents we now have at our disposal, foremost of which are the letters written by Insinger's friend Wilbour. These confirm that the Luxor house was not built until 1888, and it is evident that – before moving there – Insinger lived in his *dahabiya* (Fig. III.4), travelling along the entire course of the Egyptian Nile and occasionally venturing into the Sudan as well.

Finally, various sources suggest that Insinger was an unpleasant character, fond of intrigue and criticism,[83] and on top of that a usurer who took advantage of the poverty of the local population.[84] Even though we have to concede that Insinger may have become rather cantankerous during his later years, one has to realise that these verdicts were communicated by people like Budge and Carter: representatives of British colonialism, who were themselves trespassing the antiquities laws and obviously did not like to be reprimanded by a fellow European about it. Similar criticism was formulated by the Dutch diplomats in Cairo – who were not exactly punctual in dealing with the shipments of objects destined for the national collection of antiquities in Leiden, and frustrated Insinger's hopes regarding the appointment of a consular agent in Luxor. We may also point to the fact that Insinger could be a faithful friend, not just to the French representatives of the Service but also to the American Wilbour, the Englishman Sayce, the Dutch museum director Pleyte, or the Egyptian Mohammed Mohassib. That he likewise made a lasting impression on the Egyptian population is proved by the fond memories of *Abu Shanab* circulating in Nubia, long after the events they purported to record. Certainly, the Leiden Museum of Antiquities will always agree with Wilbour's statement: 'Insinger is a true friend.'[85]

---

79 Wilson 1964, 102, 223; James 1992, 76; Bierbrier 2012, 273.
80 It should be pointed out that Insinger is never mentioned as a Luxor dealer of antiquities in the various editions of the Baedeker guidebooks; see Hagen/Ryholt 2016, Appendix 3.
81 Wilson 1964, 102.
82 Bierbrier 2012, 273.
83 This transpires from the article in *The Egyptian Gazette* quoted by Budge 1920, 367; James 1992, 78.
84 Algemeen Rijksarchief (National Archives), The Hague, Correspondence with the diplomatic office in Egypt and the general consulate at Alexandria, 1861-1884, 2.05.38/1497, letter of 5 April 1906.
85 Quoted by Capart 1936, 409.

Appendix I: List of acquisitions from Insinger

Abbreviations: LR = RMO archives, letters received, LD = RMO Archives, letters dispatched, LI = letters written by Insinger (see Appendix II)

inv.nos.	date	description	documentation
AES 1-6	1882	Coptic pottery, flint implements	LR 1882/97, 101 LD 1882/136-137, 142, 146
AES 7-9	1882	2 stelae, 1 Archaic Period bowl	LI 1-2 LR 1882/132, 135, 194, 208, 214, 242-243; 1883/115 LD 1882/240-241, 301, 320, 324, 354
AES 40	1886	92 Coptic manuscripts	LI 4-5 = LR 1885/165, 1886/11 LR 1886/70 LD 1885/201, 1886/55, 93, 95, 100
AES 12-b-15-b	1886	2 mummies, 1 cartonnage, 2 coffins	LI 6-9 = LR 1886/44, 88, 100; 1887/38 LR 1886/77; 1887/42 LD 1886/104, 107, 128, 177; 1887/21, 54
AES 16-b-173	1888	6 pots, 132 ostraca, textiles	LI 8, 10-11 = LR 1886/100; 1888/17, 52 LR 1888/54, 57 LD 1886/177; 1888/40, 63, 67, 73
F 95/5.1	1895	Papyrus Insinger	LI 17-25 = LR 1895/10, 32, 62, 67, 69-70, 74, 88, 99 LD 1895/31, 79, 81, 92, 143-146
F 95/8.5-13	1895	linseed, textiles	LI 8, 10, 27 = LR 1886/100, 1888/17, 1895/176 LD 1895/211
F 97/6.1-732	1897	732 ostraca	LI 17, 22, 29, 31-34 = LR 1895/10, 70; 1896/131; 1897/34, 79, 105, 119 LR 1897/91, 97, 100 LD 1896/169, 185; 1897/41, 71, 118, 124, 129, 151
F 99/1.1-484	1899	1 inscription fragment, 3 stamped bricks, 481 ostraca	LI 35-40 = LR 1898/73, 97, 127, 150, 170a; 1899/52 LR 1898/215; 1899/2, 15, 21, 30, 34 LD 1898/97-98; 1899/15, 29, 35, 40
F 1901/1.1-330	1901	prehistory, pottery, glass, figurines, 247 ostraca	LI 40-47 = LR 1899/52; 1900/44, 67, 173, 177, 184, 198, 240 LR 1900/238 LD 1900/91, 196
F 1901/9.1-293	1901	prehistory, pottery, figurines, 128 ostraca	LI 46-47, 49-50 = LR 1900/198, 240; 1901/14, 135 LR 1901/181-182 LD 1901/169, 175, 185, 190
F 1929/12.1-78	1929	sculpture, figurines, pottery, textiles, ethnography	LR from C.A.S. Insinger-Everwijn Lange, 5-12-1929, 10-9 and 29-10-1930, 14-7-1933 LD 7-12 and 13-12-1929, 26-8 and 23-10-1930
F 1941/4.1	1941	1 pot	LR from C.A.S. Insinger-Everwijn Lange, 10-9-1930
F 1956/10.1-7	1956	7 mummies and mummy parts	LR from J.H.O. Insinger, 8-10 and 19-10- 1956 LD 17-10 and 24-10-1956
F 1957/11.3-4	1957	1 forged papyrus roll, 1 pot	LR from J.H.O. Insinger, 18-11-1957 LD 14-11 and 22-11-1957
F 1984/1.1-238	1929 (sic)	238 Roman coins	LI 37-39, 41 = LR 1898/127, 150, 170a; 1900/44 LD 1900/91

Appendix II: Translations of letters written by Insinger

1. To Pleyte – RMO Archives 19.7.2/1: archives Pleyte, correspondence

Dear Sir!

Today I am sending by mail a parcel to your address, including some photographs I made this winter in Egypt; though unfortunately in most cases the execution remained less than mediocre, partly due to the difficulty of lighting the tombs by means of a mirror, I believe that they have at least the merit of not yet having been made by others.

I also have the honour to inform you that one of these days I shall be sending several items to the Netherlands, to be remitted to you afterwards, including two stelae – the first and smaller one bought by Mr Schelling at el Kab, and probably originally from there; the other, larger one bought by me at Thebes, and probably deriving from Abydos – which we have the honour hereby to present to you.

Mr Maspero, who has seen the smaller one, thought it was either authentic or an imitation of the Roman period, because during a rapid inspection he thought he could discern traces of older work.

Hoping that there may be some interest in it for you, I have the honour to call myself with all respect,

Yours faithfully,
J.H. Insinger
Pegli
10 June 1882

2. To Pleyte – RMO Archives 19.7.2/1: archives Pleyte, correspondence

Dear Sir!

With reference to your valued letter to my brother of about 2 months ago, I take the liberty to point out to you that only the largest stone belongs to me, the other being a present from A.J. Schelling of Nieuwerkerk aan den IJssel. He also sent a small stone bowl from the tombs opposite Girgeh, which made Mr Maspero jealous because Bulak only has some sherds, no complete specimen. I wrote my brother about it, but do not know whether it arrived complete.

I thought to understand from your letter, which I received only a short while ago, that you regarded <u>both</u> stones as coming from me, and therefore you will not take this small rectification ill.

In case I shall return to Egypt I hope to make some more photographs. Buying will be difficult with the masses of Englishmen, and importing even more so.

With all respect I have the honour to call myself,
Yours faithfully,
J.H. Insinger
Napels
16 Oct 1882

3. To Pleyte – RMO Archives 19.7.2/1: archives Pleyte, correspondence
(copy in RMO Archives 17.1.2/30: letters received 1884, no. 94)

Dear Sir!

I have been requested by somebody who prefers not to do it directly himself, and who does not want his name to be mentioned overmuch (Brugsch, the curator here), to offer a collection of cloth and textile found on Egyptian mummies, from the Vth dynasty to the Coptic period, and including the various kinds of textile in which the mummies of the pharaohs were wrapped.

The collection consists of 250 different specimens, 10 x 10 centimeters, neatly mounted on paper with reference to the provenance. To be sent as collis postal.

The price asked is 50 Napoleons[1] (slightly under 500.- Dutch florins)

Though of course it is rather sensitive to be assisting in such a transaction, I have thought passing you the information would be to the interest of the museum, because somebody else might buy the collection.

May I be permitted to add as my private opinion, that the gentleman in question is certainly able in his position to put such a collection together, that I have seen that

---

[1] French gold coin minted in various denominations from 5 to 100 francs.

pieces of cloth have been removed from the back of the royal mummies, and that finally I do not believe that this gentleman would dare to cheat us.

In case the museum agrees to the offer, and I could be of further assistance (B preferred not to write himself) I am completely at your service, and would request you to address your letters to J.H.I., poste restante, Cairo, Egypt.

With all respect I have the honour to be,
Yours faithfully,
J.H. Insinger
Cairo
1 June 1884

4. To Pleyte – RMO Archives 17.1.2/31: letters received 1885, no. 165

Dear Sir!

After the purchase of Coptic manuscripts by the Austrian crown-prince in the Fayum[2] people have started excavations in other places, because it seems that most of them were buried, either separately or together with corpses, in times of persecutions of the Christians. They have been bought for France, and I have also succeeded to secure about 120 sheets, some of them rather damaged and others less so, some inscribed in black ink only, others decorated in red ink and other colours. Moreover, the finders have probably torn the sheets apart in order to sell them more easily, so that there are only fragments, even though several sheets belong to the same volume. This for a start. I showed some sheets to Mr Maspero, who was much interested in them, and to Mr Bouriant, curator at Bulaq, who translated some portions and found some sermons and an unknown gospel among them. The question is: do you want to take them over for the museum, or do you know another national institution in the Netherlands which would fancy the parchments? In that case I would relinquish them for what they cost me on average, 1 Dutch florin per sheet. Let me add however that I do this without any profit (in Paris one gives 5 francs and more per sheet) in order to ensure that the Netherlands will not lag behind, and with the necessary consequence that they will be published and translated before long. In case the State decides to purchase, I would consider it a debt of honour towards me that I shall receive at least 1 copy of the publication.

---

2 This refers to the 1883 acquisition by Erzherzog Rainer (not the crown prince but a nephew of the Emperor Franz I; see Bierbrier 2012, 454) of a collection of 10,000 papyri from Arsinoe in the Fayum, which he would donate to the Austrian National Library in 1899.

The shipment would be sufficiently simple; by parcel-post under a fictitious statement of contents to my brother W.A. Insinger in the Netherlands, and from him to you.

With all respect I have the honour to call myself,
Yours faithfully,
J.H. Insinger
Balliana
9 Dec 1885

Address: poste restante Cairo, Egypt
The parchments are most probably from Der-el Ahmar, the Red Monastery near Sohag.

5. To Leemans – RMO Archives 17.1.2/32: letters received 1886, no. 11

Dear Professor!

Yesterday I received with great pleasure your missive dated 24 Dec. and as a consequence I have the honour to inform you that one of these days I shall be sending a tin case holding the parchments in question to my brother W.A. Insinger (c/o Pijnenburg, Lage-Vuursche). Regarding the publication, this was and is of course no more than a request within the framework of what is possible, and if they prove to be really interesting. I therefore consider your answer as a statement from your side that everything possible will be done, and matters will not be hushed up. Should it later be desirable to remit them to another institution, then this would only prove to me that this other institution values them, in other words that they are not devoid of interest.

I can also inform Your Honour regarding the price, that you will find more than 120 sheets; properly counted there are about 150; however, upon consultation of my notes I proved to have spent merely £ 12, say 120 Dutch florins, and in exchange for that remuneration they will be at the State's disposal.

As far as other antiquities are concerned I can briefly report to Your Honour the following: various spots are occasionally being excavated, in particular nowadays Thebes and Akhmim, often by private parties. Half of the finds go to the Bulaq museum, half to the excavators. These excavators, almost exclusively natives, do the work on the basis of speculation, sell their share, and for these items Mr Maspero then gives off a billet de laisser passer for the customs (in fact all export is prohibited). Moreover, the museum exchanges and sells unwanted objects acquired in this manner or from its own excavations, in order to increase the small budget to a certain extent.

I shall probably soon meet Mr Maspero in Luxor and ask him all informations. There is also another method: in spite of excellent supervision people do a lot of secret digging and bring it to the market in Luxor. In most places, especially in Luxor, all nations down to the lowest in rank have consular agents who do nothing except giving parties for the tourists and buying antiquities on behalf of such countries. The Netherlands have <u>nobody anywhere</u>. One of the best dealers in antiquities at Luxor, by chance a rather decent man (O, rara avis!) whom I have never been able to catch with forged antiquities, wanted very much to become agent for the Netherlands, and was prepared to give a generous gift to Leiden in order to realise this. I told him this would depend of his decency, that perhaps he would be requested to make purchases and expected to serve the State courteously. I shall write our Consul General about it, and hope and expect that – if needed – Your Honour will exert some pressure, so that your museum's interests will be strongly represented.

Other news I can report to Your Honour is that the presence of the Englishmen in Egypt really has a certain benefit: the soldiers of the Sudan Expedition who have to serve a disciplinary punishment (both Englishmen and Egyptians) are being employed in cleaning the island of Philae. What I saw of it yesterday gave me the very best impression; they have also worked in a passage which seems to be leading under the branch of the Nile to the island of Bigheh lying opposite, but it is full of mud. After working there for a while the pumps got blocked, but there seems to be a plan to resume the work later with better pumps.

One is also digging at Kubbet el Hawwa, <u>a little</u> to the North of Aswan, on the west bank, and seems to have discovered the necropolis of Aswan there, under the sand covering the mountain of sandstone.[3]

With all respect, Dear Professor, I have the honour to call myself,
Yours faithfully,
J.H. Insinger
Aswan
12 Jan 1886

---

3   This, and the preceding remark on work at Philae, concerns the excavations directed by Francis Algernon Wallace, Baron Grenfell (1841-1925), commander-in-chief of the Egyptian army. See Bierbrier 2012, 226; Maspero 1887b, 227-234.

6. To Leemans – RMO Archives 17.1.2/32: letters received 1886, no. 44

Dear Professor!

As I presume, the Coptic parchments will already have reached you. I tried to buy more in Akhmim, but the prices had gone up too much. The bibliothèque nationale paid fr 4.- to fr 6.- per sheet, and 20 sheets for the British Museum were bought for £ 16. However, it is probable that similar parchments will also be sold next year at other places, and then for less money.

Your Honour asked what was sold by the Bulaq museum? Mr Maspero answered: at the moment hardly anything but various ushebti; about 150 types for 1 to ½ francs each on average; those from deïr-el-bahari, the beautiful blue royal ones, for fr 10.- on average.

L. mummies from Akhmim.

While we stayed there, I asked him to cede me two good ones, in order to hand them over to Leyden if one wished so. There were two of them, of which the half that was the finders' share had been estimated as 7 £, and Mr M. let me have them together for 8 £. I shall keep them at your disposal for that price plus the costs of packing (in case of need they can be packed by the museum carpenter, who is used to such work).

With all respect I have the honour to call myself,
Yours faithfully,
J.H. Insinger
Siut
21 March 1886

p.s.
Mr Maspero assured me he would like to do anything which would please the museum or Your Honour personally. If Your Honour would for instance want other mummies, or extra ones (always from Akhmim), or if duplicates of other material would arrive from elsewhere, he would deal with that either directly or through my offices.

7. To Leemans – RMO Archives 17.1.2/32: letters received 1886, no. 88

Dear Professor!

Some months ago I sent Your Honour a letter which, apparently, did not reach its destination. Indeed, I heard from Mr A Heemskerk here, the son of the Secretary of State, that he had been requested by his father to look out for mummies on behalf of the museum. Now in my letter I informed Your Honour that 1st the Bulaq museum sells mummies, 2nd that I had already taken over 2 mummies at Akhmim, by the mediation of Mr Maspero, together for £ 8 (Dfl. 96.-), taken them on board of my ship, and, because at that price they were rather cheap, held them at the museum's disposition for a certain time, but would otherwise send them to one of my relatives.

Next I drew Your Honour's attention to the circumstance that the only means to acquire antiquities from Luxor would be the appointment of a consular agent there, for which I would be able to suggest one of the best local antiquities dealers. Indeed this is how other nations buy their objects and have them shipped. However, in that case Your Honour would have to approach the Foreign Secretary, as our local Consul general, Mr Van der Does de Willebois, told me he would be willing to appoint somebody, but only if the initiative comes from The Hague at your recommendation.

The aim of the present this letter, however, is mainly to inform you that Mr Grébaud, the newly appointed Director of the museum here instead of Mr Maspero who asked to be discharged, told me that he intends to sell a lot of things from the museum here, which are not needed according to his opinion. I shall not offer an opinion to which extent this is right, but did not want to refrain from pointing out to you this potential opportunity of acquiring very interesting items for Leiden at a cheap price perhaps, that may fill lacunas in several things, irrespective of their real value here.

With all respect I have the honour to call myself,
Yours faithfully,
J.H. Insinger
Cairo
24 June 1886

8. To Leemans – RMO Archives 17.1.2/32 – letters received 1886, no. 100

Dear Professor!

Answering Your Honour's of June 15 and July 15, which I received 14 days after each other, I have the honour to report to you.

1st that I intend to have the mummies packed one of these days at Bulaq, and I shall then discuss the best way of shipping it with Mr Reckers, Vice Consul and Deputy Consul-General.

2nd as regards a short description of items which are for sale at the museum, I spoke with Mr Grébaud and received His Honour's promise to that effect, and I also urged the Second Curator, Mr Bouriant, to take care that the matter will not be forgotten but will be dealt with as soon as possible. Among others, there are several Old Kingdom statues, somewhat damaged but I think Leiden has no such things and they would be available for a very reasonable price. Stelae, also Old Kingdom, and some remaining ushebti from Deïr el Bahari. Mr Grébaud also assured me that he personally would like to do for you, the nestor of Egyptologists, whatever you might request of him, and that he would answer with the greatest pleasure any questions or informations which you might desire to address to him.

Then I take the liberty to inform you that I participated in the unwrapping of most mummies from Deïr el-Bahari, that I took numerous photographs, and as soon as I shall find some time to print them, I shall send to Your Honour, and to the museum of ethnography, prints of my photographs and copies of the ethnographic measurements.

As you presumed, thousands of corpses have been found at Akhmim; only several hundreds of these were in coffins; and about 100 of them rather complete. As always, a lot of this has been exaggerated. Stelae, amulets, etc. were rather rare, though the coptic bodies had lots of ingeniously woven textiles, that could be acquired for nothing but are terribly expensive now. Though I almost missed the opportunity, I possess some specimens, together with some samples of cloth of the Deïr-el Bahari mummies. When I have managed to get them somewhat flat, and a good opportunity presents itself, I shall probably send them to the museum via my brother.

Enclosed Your Honour will find the inscription on the first coffin, and that on the cartonnage; of the other about half the first line; this coffin still seems to have been completely open,[4] and I left it as it was.

With all respect I have the honour to call myself,
Yours faithfully,
J.H. Insinger
Cairo
15 July 1886
[*enclosed one sheet with text copies and brief descriptions*]

9. To Leemans – RMO Archives 17.1.2/33: letters received 1887, no. 38

Dear Sir!

Already while shipping the 2 mummies I wrote to my brother W.A. Insinger, Pijnenburg, Lage-Vuursche, to ask the museum for the £ 8 only. Because of the meagre funding at the museum's disposal I shall not charge it with the expenses of packing etc. If I would not be unwell, I

---

4   Perhaps the word 'not' was omitted here, and Insinger means that the coffin was still unopened.

would have sent the promised photographs earlier on. Please forgive postcard.

Yours faithfully,
J.H. Insinger
Assuan
14 Feb 1887

10. To Leemans – RMO Archives 17.1.2/34: letters received 1888, no. 17

Dear Sir!

During all the years that I was in Egypt, I aimed my photographic object-lens at inscriptions etc. in numerous places where nobody else did so. Due to many causes which are easy to explain, the negatives are often bad: I have to print them myself as I do not dare to entrust my negatives to anybody. Photographically speaking the results are generally very bad. Yet Prof. Erman,[5] who asked for a series for the costs of printing, flatters me to such an extent; Maspero makes use of them in his Archéologie Egyptienne, and in his planned publication Histoire d'Egypte,[6] so that I start believing they have some documentary value. True, it is only piece-work; in many sites there are lacunas because I lost the negatives; other sites have not been fully recorded. But the monuments are disappearing so quickly these last 10 years; all scholars, from Lepsius[7] onwards, have committed such errors, that a photographic document here and there is perhaps not unwelcome. Moreover, even the Kheops pyramid consists merely of building-stones. If one amateur or another would follow my example, and donate his photographs to museums, there would at least be a complete record here and there.

Thus I plan to print my complete collection; what ranges as views of the land and the people goes to the Geographical Society; a few ethnographical ones to the museum therefor; I shall send the archaeological ones to the museum of antiquities in Leyden, where perhaps they can find a place in the library. As I have to fight my way through 6 to 7 hundred negatives, and am sailing up the Nile again, some time will pass before the full collection will be present. Today the first group leaves as registered mail.

Please allow me the advice, based on experience: if the photographs will be mounted, have them stuck at the 4 corners only; this ensures the preservation of the silver print.

One of these days you will receive via my brother W.A. Insinger, or perhaps you have already received, upon payment of the costs of transport: textiles from Akhmim, wrappings of the Pharaohs and others, and ostraca, mainly from Karnak.

Hoping to be informed by Your Honour of the safe arrival of these various items, I have the honour to call myself with all respect,

Yours faithfully,
J.H. Insinger
Siut
6 Jan 1888

11. To Pleyte (?) – RMO Archives 17.1.2/34: letters received 1888, no. 52 [copy]

[Dear Sir!]

Today I received your two letters. I can tell the Director of the museum that I shall be writing my brother about the ostraca and the textiles from Akhmim, and will dispatch as registered mail today: 84 photographs. I possess between 6 and 700 negatives, but only the archaeological ones will go to Leiden, the geographical or ethnographical ones to the Geographical Society or the Ethnographic museum.

I have to write to Mr Leemans that at the moment I am in Luxor. I left Cairo in the first days of December, but did not stay much in town [etc. etc. etc.]

Yours faithfully,
J.H. Insinger
Luxor
2 March 1888

---

5   Adolf Erman (1854-1937), German Egyptologist, director of the Egyptian department of the Berlin Museum; see Bierbrier 2012, 180-181.
6   For Insinger's photos in these two publications (Maspero 1887a; Maspero 1895-1897), cf. Raven 1991, ns. 78-79. See also p. 13 n. 14 above.
7   Karl Richard Lepsius (1810-1884), German Egyptologist, editor of the lithographic atlases of the Denkmäler aus Aegypten und Aethiopien (Berlin 1849-1859). See Bierbrier 2012, 324-326.

12. To Leemans – RMO Archives 17.1.2/34: letters received 1888, no. 107

Dear Sir!

If possible I would like to receive notice of the northernmost photographs I sent Your Honour; I think I got as far as Abydos; thus I could continue the series. I think my last consignment was 7 to 8 weeks ago.

With all respect
Yours faithfully
J.H. Insinger
Cairo
8 June 1888

13. To Pleyte (?) – RMO Archives 17.1.2/34: letters received 1888, no. 121 [copy]

[Dear Sir!]

I hasten to answer your kind letter of June 22. I do not live [etc. etc.]
    Yesterday I dispatched 81 photographs to your address. The Bulaq museum will follow. There do not seem to be many opportunities to enrich the museum. For that, money would have to be available and a representative here. It is surprising how much other countries spend. Dr Schweinfurt,[8] about whom you wrote, though not an Egyptologist, almost has a blank cheque for Germany and makes use of it.
    I do not believe that the market scene (representation on Ancient Eg. monument and published by Lepsius in his great work) is known;[9] there were few inscriptions. The best proof lies in the exchange of goods (barter) between the person who sits below, in front of the people behind their baskets, and the standing person. Even now the market in Upper Egypt is similar; long rows of dealers, each behind his few products for sale. In those ...[10] writing a lot, this probably is the village-hall where the chief of police and the tax collector keep office on market days.

With best wishes for [etc. etc.]
[Yours faithfully]
J.H. Insinger
Cairo
5 July 1888

14. To Leemans – RMO Archives 17.1.2/34: letters received 1888, no. 143

Dear Sir!

Yesterday I sent Your Honour 60 photographs by mail, as registered printed matter. I think the museum now has all my photographs as far as they concern Ancient Egyptian subjects. In case I shall make more negatives later, I hope to send you prints of them.
    Mr Grébaud informed me, now that the Bulaq museum is selling its duplicates, that it includes some items for which it would be a pity if they ended up in private collections instead of museums, and he requested me to draw your attention to this.

With all respect I have the honour to call myself,
Yours faithfully,
J.H. Insinger
Cairo
25 July 1888

15. To Pleyte – RMO Archives 17.1.2/40: letters received 1894, no. 70

Dear Sir!

For years I have been collecting photographs – some purchased, some taken myself – with the result that I possess perhaps one of the most extensive collections of photographs of Egypt, as well as a large number of Syria, Italy, etc. You will find some reproductions of them in the most recent publications of the work by the French archaeological missions here, as well as in the forthcoming publication by Maspero.[11] Even so, a lot remains unpublished. Here my collection is being destroyed by moths. I want to send it to Holland, and thought that you would perhaps find it more desirable to keep it in the museum than locked away with my brother or another relative where it would be hard to see. I therefore propose you to receive the collection on loan to the museum.
    Of course, there are quite a few photos among them of ships, people, landscapes which are of no importance whatever for you. As I have stuck them on sheets of cardboard with running numbers, I can hardly take them out.
    Should my proposal please you, then I would like to hear further details from you regarding: manner of shipping; duration of loan, etc., etc. In case some of it will be published, I would however desire a copy of the

---

8 Georg August Schweinfurth (1836-1925), German explorer and botanist who settled in Cairo in 1875. See Bierbrier 2012, 497.
9 Probably this refers to a scene depicted in the tomb of Fetekta at Abusir; see Lepsius 1849-1859, II, pl. 96; Porter/Moss 1974, 351, tomb LS 1, scene (6)b.
10 Here the text of the original letter seems to have been illegible.

11 See above, p. 65 n. 6.

printed matter, and if it would be one of my own photos, my name should be mentioned.

With all respect I have the honour to call myself,
Yours faithfully,
J.H. Insinger
Luxor
20 March 1894

16. To Pleyte – RMO Archives 17.1.2/40: letters received 1894, no. 242

Dear Sir!

Due to circumstances beyond my control the shipment of my photographs has been delayed. They have now arrived in Cairo on October 28, and will be sent on to you by the good services of Mr Kurtas, Chancellor at the Consulate. You will find them mounted on sheets, with consecutive n^{os} from 1 to 1050; of these the n°s 662-664, 695, 701, 702 & 859 are missing. Since these mainly depict views of the Netherlands or portraits of acquaintances, I thought they had better stay with me than in Leiden.

Moreover, there is a roll with some unmounted photos, for which I had no cardboard, and some of which may be duplicates. It has been written on the reverse below.

To my regret I cannot meet your request to mark those photos which have been published; they are in the recueil de la mission du Caire, histoire ancienne des peuples d'Orient Maspero;[12] and because they have many prints of mine I do not know what they already gave to the printer; and some in the archéologie,[13] and Ancient Egypt and Assyria,[14] both by Maspero. My own photos, some 9 x 13, almost all 13 x 18, have been marked with an I; the others have been purchased or exchanged and are not my literary property.

Hoping to be informed of the safe arrival, I remain with all respect,
Yours faithfully,
J.H. Insinger
Luxor
18 Nov 1894

---

12 The first mentioned title is the journal *Recueil de travaux relatifs à la philologie et l'archéologie égyptienne et assyrienne: pour servir de bulletin à la mission française du Caire*, which appeared from 1870 onwards. The second title is Maspero 1895-1897 (first edition 1875) ; cf. Raven 1991, n. 78 and cf. p. 13 n. 14 above.
13 Maspero 1887a; see Raven 1991, n. 79.
14 English translation of Maspero 1895-1897.

P.S.
Regarding the purchase of antiquities, Mr Leemans already wrote me previously about it, but he requested a full report about the object, copies of the inscriptions, price, etc. This, however, is impossible. An object is offered for sale, one either buys or does not buy, and two days later it may have been acquired by a tourist, or a dealer from Cairo or similar. Sometimes one can considerably lower the price by just waiting, sometimes this trick does not work at all and another person makes a higher bid. Two days ago a ship arrived here with the limestone door frame of a tomb, the pieces a and b (c was missing).

Probably it had been a tomb of unfired brick, or the rock had been bad, and these were pièces rapportées. It was for an official of Usortesen.[15] Pieces with that royal name do not often occur, especially not from this area (findspot Erment, Gebeleen or Mealla). The owner refused £ 2; but one would have had it for £ 2 ½. Now the dealer will ask at least £ 10. Can you tell me what kind of objects you want, or from which period (if that can be defined), and open a credit for me, then I shall do my best to make sure the museum does not pay too much; other conditions are impracticable.

With all respect,
J.H. Insinger
Luxor
18 Nov 1894

17. To Pleyte – RMO Archives 17.1.2/41: letters received 1895, no. 10

Mr Pleyte, Esq
Director, National Museum of Antiquities

In possession of your honoured letter n° 304 I take the liberty to ask Your Honour if your honoured letter has to serve as receipt and proof in case *e.g.* my heirs should want to have the photographs back in their possession (this is not probable in my own case).

Regarding your letter n° 285 I can inform you that I already bought some potsherds with demotic inscriptions; and that somebody wrote me from Akhmim about two demotic papyri, wide 30 cm; total length 5 m: I asked

---

15 Senwosret or Sesostris, name of three of the kings of Dynasty XII (1939-1760 BC).

him to copy the beginning, if possible, to mention the price, etc., and shall then send you further information.

With all respect I have the honour to call myself,
Yours faithfully,
J.H. Insinger
Luxor
4 Jan 1895

18. To Pleyte – RMO Archives 17.1.2/41: letters received 1895, no. 32

Mr W. Pleyte, Esq
Director, National Museum of Antiquities
Leiden

Mr A. Frenay, Consular Agent of France in Akhmim, Upper Egypt, possesses a demotic papyrus, high 30 cm, in two parts, long according to him about 4 ½ metres; according to Mr Legrain, inspector of the museum of Gizeh, it is probably longer; the first lines "traitent de la morale."

One is negotiating about it for France. Price fr 4000.- (four thousand francs). Perhaps one could get a bit off, but I believe only a little.

Your Honour could do as you please: either correspond with that gentleman himself, or with me, or, if Your Honour should be afraid that somebody else would forestall you, simply send me a telegram. I can also tell you that Mr Legrain confessed he did not have the money required to conclude the bargain.

With all respect,
Yours faithfully,
J.H. Insinger
Luxor
10 Feb 1895

19. To Pleyte – RMO Archives 17.1.2/41: letters received 1895, no. 62 (telegram, 9 April 1895)

Pleyte
Leiden
Paysbas
Expediez argent ou papyrus perdu.
Insinger

20. To Pleyte – RMO Archives 17.1.2/41: letters received 1895, no. 67

Dear Sir !

After your telegram of March 15 I immediately wrote to Mr A. Frenay. However, I waited in vain for further notice and especially for the remittance. Finally Frenay gave me presumption[16] till the last day of this month, and yesterday I telegraphed to you: send money, or papyrus lost. Indeed, here in Egypt the custom is cash payment for antiquities, or at least cheque. Now your letter arrived yesterday evening. Today I wrote to Frenay, that if needed I shall buy the papyrus myself, and shall then give him a promissory note for a few months (no private person in Upper Egypt keeps f 2000,- in cash at home), and to Mr Van den Does de Willebois with the request to send the papyrus, should he receive it from Frenay or from me, to you either directly or via the Foreign Office, since this is always done for the English and French museums; now I hope it will be possible for you to remit the fl 2000,- as soon as possible, preferably to me, since I took the responsibility vis-à-vis Frenay. Fl 2000,- is a little more than fr 4000. However, I asked v.d.D. de Willebois to charge me for the costs of transport and if possible the <u>insurance</u>, and I think that I can also charge my telegram of yesterday to the State, now 81 piaster of yesterday, about f 10.12. As soon as Frenay accepts my proposal, or the papyrus will be sent, I shall inform you. Another reason that also forces me to urge for speedy remittance is that I think I shall leave from here for the Netherlands in the first days of June, but I do not know how long I shall be en route and correspondence would therefore become very difficult.

With all respect,
Yours faithfully,
J.H. Insinger
Luxor
10 April 1895

21. To Pleyte – RMO Archives 17.1.2/41: letters received 1895, no. 69

Dear Sir!

On the evening of the day before yesterday, 8 telegraphic money orders of £E 154.- arrived here. The post office did not have that amount here. I immediately sent a telegram to Frenay, shall also write to him today, and hope to be able to inform you by the following mail that the papyrus

---

16   For 'prorogation'?

is on its way to Leiden via Mr v.d. Does. And upon arrival I hope we shall be able to congratulate each other with the new acquisition.

With all respect,
Yours faithfully,
J.H. Insinger
Luxor
12 April 1895

22. To Pleyte – RMO Archives 17.1.2/41: letters received 1895, no. 70

Dear Sir!

Just in time to send it along with the boat, I am receiving the enclosed telegram of Mr Frenay. When Mr Van den Does complies with the request which I made to him, and immediately sends on the papyrus with the valise diplomatique, then I reckon the papyrus could be in the Hague within 10 to 12 days.

After the receipt of the £E 154.- I shall check at the office how much more or less it will be than the fr. 4000.-, and if I receive a bill from Mr v.d. Does I shall send it along to you. I suppose that the money which you remitted by telegraphic order does not come directly from the national treasury, and that you have to write a declaration for it. It will probably help to obtain a speedy financial arrangement if you send me a form to be filled in or copied by me.

Before the arrival of the tourists I bought some more potsherds; now that they have left again I shall be able to continue the purchases; as they are paid between 8 for a piaster (12 ½ cent) to a maximum of 2 piasters a piece for larger specimens, it will in fact only be the shipment which will cost the museum something worth mentioning; perhaps one of the Dutch ships will carry them for free.

With all respect I have the honour to remain,
Yours faithfully,
J.H. Insinger
Luxor
12 April 1895

[enclosed telegram, 12 April 1895]
Reçu enverrai demain papyrus comme indiqué prière diriger argent Anglo Egyptian Bank Alexandrie à mon compte merci Frenay

23. To Pleyte – RMO Archives 17.1.2/41: letters received 1895, no. 74

Dear Sir!

After having informed Mr v.d. Does de Willebois, our Consul General & political Agent, that the papyrus would be addressed to him, and having concluded the sale with Frenay, I received telegrams from him, requesting not to address to him and to wait for a letter. After having telegraphed to Frenay, the papyrus proved to be en route to the C.G. Since I know positively that England, France and Germany always act in the same manner, I do not know what the C.G. wants. Shall send you more information as soon as I get it, but in the meantime am curious what the C.G. will do with this national property. Perhaps a letter from you via the Hague, urging the C.G. to assist Leiden, would not be improper.

With all respect,
J.H. Insinger
Luxor
14 April 1895

24. To Pleyte – RMO Archives 17.1.2/41: letters received 1895, no. 88

Dear Sir,

Due to great lack of care of the postal service, the letters from Mr v.d. Does de Willebois, though sent to me by registered mail, only came into my possession yesterday evening. H.E. is of the opinion that the museum direction knows very well that the papyrus has been purchased, and has been sent to him, which I can totally confirm; that, as the Consul General has no valise diplomatique – unlike the French, English, etc. – he cannot send otherwise than any private person, so that a package may very well be undone or broken by accident, and if the papyrus would then be uncovered, both H.E. and our government would be put in a very difficult position.

That it is possible that if you ask an export license, it would be refused.

Now I shall probably go to Europe at the beginning of June but I run a major risk of visitation; moreover I consider going via Constantinopel, where I might also run into difficulties.

Therefore I shall send to Mr v.d.D. a request for export addressed to Mr de Morgan; if it will be permitted, all is well, and if not I shall look for alternatives without compromising myself. Now that I know all, I feel forced to declare that I can only approve the procedure of Mr van den Does; without the explanation of the letters, his telegrams gave me the impression that H.E. did not want to cooperate, though the opposite proves to be the case. Unfortunately, all of this causes a major delay; the papyrus is now in Cairo, I received the avis de reception from the post office.

It is deplorable that we do not have a Consular agent <u>here</u>, a native just like the other nations, who helps the people in a cheap way. The person I have in mind, the most honest dealer in antiquities, now possesses several demotic contracts again.

With all respect
J.H. Insinger
Luxor
22 April 1895

25. To Pleyte – RMO Archives 17.1.2/41: letters received 1895, no. 99

Dear Sir!

Yesterday evening I received by postcard information from Mr. v.d.Does de Willebois that the papyrus has been sent to the address of the Min. of Foreign Affairs, insured for fr. 500.-. (the postal service does not allow more)

Hoping to hear about the safe arrival soon,
Yours faithfully,
J.H. Insinger
Luxor
8 May 1895
Perhaps I can come to Leiden in July or Aug.

26. To Pleyte – RMO Archives 17.1.2/41: letters received 1895, no. 119

Dear Sir!

Yesterday evening I was most sadly shocked by the sad news of the death of Madame your wife;[17] I shall not try to write words of consolation to you, they will help you next to nothing; I myself have lost many members of my family and know from experience that the awareness that others share your loss is beneficial: rest assured of my condolences.

Probably you will finally have received the papyrus by now; I sincerely hope that it is satisfactory; of course I would feel very sorry if, the first time that I act as an intermediary, the purchase for such a large sum would prove to be a disappointment. However, after what I heard about it here from competent people I feel rather confident.

In 14 days I hope to depart from here, probably via Constantinopel, and by the end of June, beginning of July hope to be in the fatherland, where I have not been for 16 years. The aim is to visit my relatives, especially two little daughters at school, and to put my wife and myself under medical treatment.

However, you will understand that somebody who lived for so long in Egypt and got into touch with so many archaeologists and antiquities, is very eager finally to see Leyden and Mr Pleyte for a change. If I cannot come instantly, I shall go to my brother's at Bennekom, and if requested we can arrange the financial matter by mail; otherwise in person, and it would surprise me if we could not find a means to get the f 156 and the remainder together. N.B. at least the official of the post or telegraph will probably be rebuked, because Luxor does not seem to be licensed to handle telegraphic money orders.

Mr de Morgan is expected here tomorrow or the day after, probably for the total clearance of the temple; Medinet Habou and Deïr el Bahari have almost been cleared; especially the first temple is <u>most</u> impressive, and more remarkable in details than one suspected.

Hoping soon to meet you in person,
Yours faithfully,
J.H. Insinger
Luxor
20 May 1895

27. To Pleyte – RMO Archives 17.1.2/41: letters received 1895, no. 176

Dear Sir!

I received your much esteemed letter d.d. 31 July; and note with great satisfaction that the papyrus seems to please you.

Today I shall write to my cousin Speelman in the Hague in order to find out whether he can receive us on Saturday or Sunday, 10 or 11 Aug. From there I plan then to come to Leiden. Should you prefer that I come later for some reason or other, then that would also be possible, though earlier would be difficult since I have to go to an uncle in Naarden on Wednesday & Thursday, and to Arnhem on Tuesday and Friday as I have to visit my youngest daughter there in the deaconesses' hospital – fortunately not for a serious indisposition.

As I shall leave towards the end of the month, you will understand that I would have some trouble to come

---

17 Pleyte had married Catharina Margaretha Templeman van der Hoeven in 1862; the couple had ten children. The wife died on 13 March 1895. See http://www.genealogieonline.nl/stamboom-driessen/I35745.php.

after the 25th. Unfortunately I am unable to do much; I already intended to come to Leiden from Amsterdam by the middle of July, but to my regret I was detained.

Some time ago I sent my brother some items for himself, others for the museum. As we found out now, various samples of mummy wrappings are still here which were in fact meant to go to the museum. I took part in the opening of the royal mummies, and everybody was allowed to take some fragments. You will find names on some of the packages; other textiles were loose, and I can only state that they come from Thebes. These items will be sent by mail to your address either today or tomorrow.

Taking pleasure in the prospect of seeing you soon, I have the honour to call myself,
Yours faithfully,
J.H. Insinger
Bennekom
3 July 1895

28. To Pleyte – RMO Archives 17.1.2/41: letters received 1895, no. 182 (telegram)

Arriving tomorrow 8.56 could I pass by the museum reply
Bible Hotel
Insinger
Amsterdam
9 August 1895

29. To Pleyte – RMO Archives 17.1.2/42: letters received 1896, no. 131

Dear Sir!

People are now rooting up the ruins of Karnak, in order to use the poussière des siècles as fertilizer on the fields, and what remains are the uncovered fragments of stone and potsherds. Thinking of you, I have therefore put a man at work, paying him so far for complete sherds 3 for 1 piaster, for broken ones 4 for 1 piaster (1 piaster = 12 ½ cent), and promising up to 15 piasters a piece for large specimens; there are now ± 50 pieces, but soon I hope to have a crate full of them. But how are we going to arrange the transport? The Consul General is on leave; the deputy, in Alexandria, is somebody I do not know in person.

What the Dutch representative and the Dutch government do now on behalf of collections is so little; the encouragement experienced by private parties so equal to nothing, that one often wonders: why should one try to do anything, if one knows from the start that one will hardly get any assistance, let alone a word of gratitude. A consular agent, for instance, would be of great use here. Is it utterly impossible to get one? This winter, Germany had somebody here[18] who pretended to be measuring up the temples, which has been done better and earlier on by others, but in reality he sought to buy antiquities, or … to search for them. Probably this person will now obtain a fixed appointment and infest these regions, and he asserted he emptied an unviolated tomb of the XIth or XIIth <Dynasty> at Gebel-eên, between Erment and Esné (An.ti, see Dümichen),[19] which will now go to Berlin[20] (close to this spot I saw tombs of the XIth).

It was last year around this time that I was received in such a most affectionate manner by you and your family. Often I still think with the utmost pleasure about these few hours spent in Leyden. May I ask to give my kind regards to all those who shared the table?

Would not you make up your mind after all to come and visit us here? Now it only takes 6 to 6½ hours to come here, and there is no more than 2 to 3 hours difference with an ongoing ticket via Brindisi or Constantinopel. Last winter was most interesting, with the clearance of Deir el Bahari, Medinet Habou and Karnak, and you need not be afraid of the heat; beans and potatoes often freeze in January, and ladies sometimes don their furs.

May I be so indiscreet as to ask how it goes with translating the papyrus? Does it contain anything of interest? Or are you finding out important things about the language or the writing?

With all respect,
Yours faithfully,
J.H. Insinger
Luxor
2 August 1896

30. To Pleyte – RMO Archives 17.1.2/42: letters received 1896, no. 168

Dear Sir!

Mr de Morgan is convinced that he cannot keep everything in Egypt after all. He does not intend at all to become refractory, especially in case another museum is concerned, as he quite rightly considers that as soon as an object ends up in a museum, it has been saved for science, will sooner or later be published, and does not run the

---

18 This must refer to Ludwig Borchardt (1863-1938), German Egyptologist and architect, who was in charge of De Morgan's project to catalogue the standing monuments of Egypt from 1896-1899; see Bierbrier 2012, 68-69.
19 The reference is doubtless to Dümichen 1865-1866.
20 The contents of the intact tomb of Henuy at Gebelein was bought by Borchardt for the Berlin Museum in 1896; see Steindorff 1901, 11 ff.

same risk of destruction as objects in private collections. Probably he will help you and me as far as possible, <u>unless</u> objects are involved such as papyri, stelae, etc., objects of first rank; in those cases he considers it his duty to preserve them for the Giza museum, and to prevent exportation. He is of a most obliging and helpful character, and likes to be of assistance. Therefore, we shall easily manage to export potsherds; though I have not got a reliable person in Cairo for the actual transport, and for instance the Consulate General ought to take charge of it. I also take small fragments; they may sometimes join here or there, produce a new word, and being charged at 4 for 12 ½ cent it means that it is better left to you to discard them.

About 3 weeks ago 8 papyri from Gebel-ein were offered for sale here,[21] together with a box inlaid in precious stones which according to the dealers had a higher value than the papyri. Four of them were of a large format, and of these 1 was bilingual: Greek and demotic. The whole lot was sold to Cairo for £ 108.-. For paintings, there is a society in Amsterdam that buys at auctions, etc., and transfers them to the State when it is in cash. Could not one do something similar for Egyptian objects? I happened to have lots of cash; you might or might not be granted such a sum of money later this year; it was a question of hours, no time even for a telegram. I was so sad that I did not even go there to see the objects; now for sure they will go to Paris, London or Berlin for £ 1080.-.

With the prospect of the arrival of Mr your son, I understand that you postpone the Egyptian trip. From July 1897, or perhaps Jan. 1898, you will probably be able to travel by train to Assuan. The main abodes are still Cairo and Luxor, and perhaps there will be 3rd-class hostels in the places with temples. The Cook's tourist steamers need 3 weeks from Cairo to Assuan and back, with for an Egyptologist far too short breaks at places of interest. The public steamer halts about an hour here and there. May I advise you to come not too late in the season? Sometimes one already has days of Khamsin[22] by the end of February, and then somebody freshly imported from Europe cannot undertake a great deal. I myself would advise the earlier the better; in October it is not too hot; the Nile is still quite high, and gives everything a totally different appearance; most tourists are here Jan – Feb, and many leave already by the end of Feb. Then everything is full, and the dealers have already sold the major part.

The cholera will probably be over now; or rather, some cases will continue, and we shall enjoy it again in 1897.

Whether one will undertake a lot of clearance of temples, etc.? All the funds have been used for the Dongola expedition,[23] clearance and restoration is mainly done with the pound sterling one charges to every tourist, but whether they will come?

Then I hear all kinds of rumours about de Morgan wanting to leave. The English can hardly appoint an Englishman, and do not have anybody suitable, but as a matter of principle they do their utmost to cause trouble for every Frenchman.

Many thanks for the proofs of the papyrus. I think it will be a delight for professionals to study it with such an edition.

Kindly requesting to give all regards, I remain with all respect,
Yours faithfully,
J.H. Insinger
Luxor
27 Sept 1896

31. To Pleyte – RMO Archives 17.1.2/43: letters received 1897, no. 34

Dear Sir!

After your honoured letter d.d. 19 Sept '96 I fell gravely ill, and as it happens more often, after having recovered the answer remained in the pen. In the meantime, 1st Mr de Morgan is here now, who stated he was prepared to seal all crates with destination Leyden and provide them with a laissez passer for the customs. 2nd I wrote to Mr Macdonald, assuming he was Dutch, in Dutch which he did not understand but all the same he granted a 50% reduction. 3rd I now have ready a crate full of inscribed sherds. However, now we have to wait until Mr de Morgan will be back in Cairo, and we need somebody in Cairo who receives the crate there, brings it to the museum for the sealing formality, and sends it on to Port-Saïd. I have nobody for that. Cannot the Foreign Office charge the Consul or the Consul General with it? Those gentlemen regard such a thing as a chore, and do not like me at all for involving them in it. A circular letter from the Foreign Office would be excellent, kindly requesting the Consuls etc. to assist in general with shipments of the national collections and to take care of transferring them.

With all respect,
Yours faithfully,
J.H. Insinger
Luxor
3 Feb. 1897

---

21 For the Gebelein papyri (mostly demotic and Greek) and their dispersal, see U. Kaplony-Heckel, in: LÄ II, 449-452.
22 Sand-storms, called after the period of fifty (Ar. *khamsin*) days in spring when they are said to occur.
23 In 1896 a military expedition force under Herbert Kitchener was sent to the Sudan in order to put an end to the Mahdist revolt. After a first victory at Dongola, order was finally restored with the battle at Omdurman in 1898. *Cf.* Carstens 2014, 645-647.

32. To Pleyte – RMO Archives 17.1.2/43: letters received 1897, no. 79

Dear Sir!

Finally! I wrote about the crate to Mr v.d. Does de Willebois, our Consul General, and today it has finally gone. I spoke about it with Mr v.d.D. de Morgan, who promised to do what was needed, but now resigned. It is <u>very</u> difficult to do something for the museum, and it is rather a pity that Mr Bretschneider, our Consul in Cairo, is unable or unwilling to assist a bit more in the shipment.

In the crate you will find ± 400 sherds. There was a lot of competition this winter; I hope to find something more and better this summer, when there are no Europeans or inspectors. Costs so far: acquisition 117 piaster, transport to Cairo 33,4 piaster; total 150,4 piaster, a little less than f 18,-.

I hope to hear about the safe arrival, and also that there is something of interest among them. I was almost cheated with a group of beautiful and large but false ones. If you want them I can send them for free during a future occasion, because the cheater was of course forced to provide good ones, and to leave the forgeries behind.

With the request to give kind regards to the family and to the gentlemen of the museum, I have the honour to call myself,

Yours faithfully,
J.H. Insinger
Luxor
21 April 1897

33. To Pleyte – RMO Archives 17.1.2/43: letters received 1897, no. 105

Dear Sir!

From Mr Macdonald I received notice that the crate with potsherds has been sent to you on board the Prins Hendrik on May 9th, telling me that he leaves the cargo assessment to the direction in Amsterdam when the crate will be delivered. I remitted him his costs at fr. 3.50 at 14 piaster plus 1,5 P.E for money orders.

My travel costs by Cook's steamer, then by rail to Cairo were 33 4/10 P.E, whereas Mr v.d. Does did not tell me how much he was charged for the sealing at the museum and the transport in Cairo.

Hoping soon to hear about the safe arrival, I have the honour to call myself with all respect,

Yours faithfully,
J.H. Insinger
Luxor
20 May 1897

34. To Pleyte – RMO Archives 17.1.2/43: letters received 1897, no. 119

Dear Sir!

Your letter of the 9th already arrived here long ago, but as I was unwell, I could not possibly answer it before. This morning your money order arrived too; everything is in perfect order, and enclosed I send you the receipts. It gives me great pleasure that the whole lot has arrived so well, and that you and Mr Boeser will perhaps find some use for it. I have given order to bring me all the potsherds one can find. Probably they are without exception from Karnak. So far I have tried in vain to get some from Erment. I was assured that some large ones were found there, that may be more important as regards contents; contracts, etc. As Professor Sayce told me, who usually buys a lot of them, he had a 'meagre harvest' this year, because I had picked all of them up right under his nose.

The government, though, does not yet seem to think that it is time to do what other governments do whenever a private person has given himself trouble on behalf of several national collections.

Is Mr naval officer[24] still in the country? And do you still plan to come here this winter? Now that de Morgan is gone, everybody deplores he has left, especially the English who caused him such a lot of trouble. In fact he was rather too decent, and too much the right man in the right place for people wanting him to stay. Coming winter Loret will probably work at Ashmunēn (Hermopolis) near Roda. At least the Greek buildings there have not been destroyed until the latter half of the present century. Legrain will probably continue in Karnak, and Daressy[25] is mentioned for Luxor. One does not recognise such a temple after clearance.

Believe me, with kind regards,
Yours faithfully,
J.H. Insinger
Luxor
27 June 1897

---

24 Doubtless one of Pleyte's sons, whose temporary visit to the Netherlands was mentioned in letter no. **30**.
25 Georges Émile Jules Daressy (1864-1938), French Egyptologist, who helped in the clearing of several major temples and was curator at the Cairo Museum. See Bierbrier 2012, 142-143.

35. To Pleyte – RMO Archives 17.1.2/44: letters received 1898, no. 73

Dear Sir!

I still bought some more potsherds this year, though not many. If you might want them for the museum, I shall hand them over with pleasure at cost price. However, I do not think our consular representatives in Cairo are very eager to send them on; I myself cannot trouble anybody else to go to the museum and have the crate sealed for the Egyptian customs; I see no other solution than that either you or the Ministry should write about this to Cairo.

It will be known to you that the tomb of Amenhotep II was opened[26] (and Mr Loret is not the one to be credited for that); it was already plundered in antiquity, but I gather many things have also disappeared now. If I find some objects from that tomb here, should I buy them on behalf of Leyden? and for how much?

I am very sorry that you have not realised your intention to come here last winter. Somers Clark[27] seems to have found objects dating to before Mena, with cartouches, at El Kab; what Abydos produced seems to be extremely important. Karnak produces many surprises. It is really worthwhile to come here sometime. I hope to leave at the beginning of June and to arrive in the Fatherland by the end of that month; perhaps I shall have the pleasure of seeing you.

With all respect,
Yours faithfully,
J.H. Insinger
Luxor
23 April 1898
P.S. Has the papyrus already come out?

36. To Pleyte – RMO Archives 17.1.2/44: letters received 1898, no. 97

Dear Sir!

On the point of leaving, I just receive a letter from Consul in Cairo, by order of Consul General, advising me to wait with transport potsherds until autumn!

With all respect,
Yours faithfully,
J.H. Insinger
Luxor
2 June 1898

37. To Pleyte – RMO Archives 17.1.2/44: letters received 1898, no. 127

Dear Sir!

Unexpectedly I rang at the door of your house[28] 2 ½ weeks ago, but the maids told me that you had gone travelling and would probably not be back soon. I felt very sorry about it, because in your last letter you wrote that for the moment it is not very probable that you will visit Egypt, and the climate of the Netherlands has done me so much harm this time, that I do not expect I shall come again soon.

That so far I did not send the potsherds was caused by the enclosed letter. After getting back to Egypt I hope to find our Consular employees will be able to finish this case which for them is so extremely complicated.

In Luxor I bought a mass of Romano-Egyptian coins. I think these items have no great value for the coin cabinet. I was told they sometimes produce interesting information about place names, etc. What does Leiden say about it?

Loret made himself detested by everybody in Egypt. He is so tactless, that the English already told him: be good or go away; he chose for the first. On top of that he seems to be arrogant, stupid, and ignorant. The Philae temple will indeed be drowned,[29] in spite of what one tells outsiders; Wilson, who was appointed as supervisor on behalf of the government,[30] told me that there will be 3 metres of water. The building will certainly not be getting any better from this.

May I ask to kindly greet the family?

With all respect,
Yours faithfully,
J.H. Insinger
Arnhem
27 July 1898

---

26 For this tomb and its discovery, see Reeves 1990, 192-199; Reeves/Wilkinson 1996, 100-103. For the (probably unfounded) rumours that the tomb had been known before by the locals, and that part of its contents was robbed, see Reeves 1990, 220 n. 89. Such rumours were partly spread due to the usual British-French animosity.

27 Somers Clarke (1841-1926), English architect and archaeologist, started explorations at el-Kab in 1893. See Bierbrier 2012, 124.

28 Pleyte lived at Rapenburg 83 in Leiden. See http://dispuutpleyte.plexus.leidenuniv.nl/NL/pleyte.php.

29 As a result of the construction of the first dam at Aswan (1899-1902).

30 The engineer W.J. Wilson was Director of Reservoirs from 1898 till his death in 1900; see http://www.britishdams.org/2006conf/papers/Paper%207%20Hill.PDF.

[enclosed: letter from Consul Bretschneider dated 31 May 1898)

38. To Pleyte – RMO Archives 17.1.2/44: letters received 1898, no. 150

Dear Sir!

After your telegram I had a vague hope of seeing you in Arnhem after all. Unfortunately this did not work out.

Upon arriving here I found a large book, Coptic inscriptions Athanasy and J.H.I.[31] The publication will doubtless satisfy the scholarly world, just as everything which comes from Leyden. I hope that the contents may be such that all the effort has been rewarded. I would not know about that, being a complete layman.

The Consul and C. General are still not back in Cairo. However, one of these days I shall venture to send the potsherds. Did the earlier transport contain any useful ones?

And now about the coins. I do not like to send them to the coin cabinet. I would rather sell them. My brother W.A. Insinger at Bennekom also has a lot of them, perhaps you might also acquire those.

I am still so exhausted by the voyage that you will forgive me if this is not longer.

With all respect, and a request to kindly greet the family and Mr Boeser,
Yours faithfully,
J.H. Insinger
Luxor
24 Aug 1898

39. To Pleyte – RMO Archives 17.1.2/44: letters received 1898, no. 170a

Dear Sir!

A crate left from here with inscribed potsherds, 381 items. It also contains some forged ones that immediately stand out by their large size. For curiosity's sake I also send these, in order to show you how many people fall for them. One crate a bit more, the other a bit less; altogether 4 for a piasters, cargo to Cairo 23 piasters. I still do not know how much the Consul will spend there on sealing, etc.

These still come from Karnak. I tried in vain to secure some from Erment. Professor Sayce yearly buys what he can, also from Elephantine.

Perhaps my brother will write you directly about the coins.

Loret is back in Egypt, and will probably continue for a while as director; too bad. The Egyptologists have not returned to Egypt, so I do not know what they intend to do this winter. Probably the clearing of Karnak will be continued. A huge work, but only now one really starts to perceive how large and how special that temple was, and how wrong all plans are. Every moment the most interesting details.

I am so sorry that I could not be in the Netherlands for the festivities. I hope you received my card to congratulate you with the much deserved honours.[32]

With all respect,
Yours faithfully,
J.H. Insinger
Luxor
23 Sept 1898

40. To Pleyte – RMO Archives 17.1.2/45: letters received 1899, no. 52

Dear Sir!

Thanks for your letter d.d 2.1. I see with pleasure that the sherds etc. were not so bad. Regarding the brick of Isi.m.Keb, Wiedemann is completely right that many of that type occur at el Hibeh; but one also finds them at Gebelēn and at Salamieh, a few hours upstream from Luxor, right-hand bank, and the one in question comes from Salamieh. I saw before my own eyes how others were taken from the foundation of a well for irrigation, according to tradition one of the many old wells dating back to Roman times.

Here it is swarming with Archaeologists. Newberry[33] and Spiegelberg[34] are working for the account of Lord

---

31 This refers to Pleyte/Boeser 1897; for Athanasy, read Anastasy.

32 On 6 September 1898, a week after her 18th birthday, the Dutch Queen Wilhelmina was inaugurated as sole ruler (having been under the regency of her mother Queen Emma since the death of her father Willem III in 1890). As part of the festivities, the usual royal distinctions were distributed to prominent members of society. Among the recipients was Willem Pleyte, who received a knighthood in the order of the Dutch Lion (Hasselbach1987, 94).

33 Percy Edward Newberry (1868-1949), British Egyptologist who excavated for several wealthy patrons; see Bierbrier 2012, 402-403.

34 Wilhelm Spiegelberg (1870-1930), German Egyptologist who travelled to Egypt several times in the years 1895-1899, before he was appointed at Strasburg University; see Bierbrier 2012, 521-522.

Northhampton[35]; Carter and Naville[36] are completing the restoration and publication of Deïr el bahari. Legrain is busy clearing Karnak, and re-erecting a lot of things, thanks to an additional grant; Daressy will complete Medinet Habu, and then tackle the Ramesseum. Then there are some others of the French mission; Somers Clarke and Quibell[37] at el Kab, Loret on his way here, plus occasionally a "wild" one who is passing by.

Is Leyden not communicating with the "mission" in Caïro? You probably know that they publish a lot; and they are most generous with their books. As Bouriant is seriously ill, Chassinat[38] deputizes in the interim.

My best congratulations for Miss Pleyte for her engagement. Yet another peaceful Germanisation.[39]

With all respect,
Yours faithfully,
J.H. Insinger
Luxor
15 Feb 1899
Now everything is expensive due to the tourists. Should I try to buy some prehistoric pots etc. this summer?

41. To Pleyte – RMO Archives 17.1.2/46: letters received 1900, no. 44

Dear Sir!

May I kindly remind you that so far I did not yet receive the money advanced for the last shipment of sherds 484/4 121 piaster + 23 cargo.

I already bought some complete pots, of the kind described by de Morgan as prehistoric.[40] However, I shall wait with the transport until I have some more, and want to try and get some of the special kind decorated with primitive ships. I could not yet secure any of those specimens.

The sherds described by you as either Meroitic or forgeries are <u>forgeries</u>. I have now learned better to distinguish them. Old pieces of sherds are inscribed in a mixture of charred palm leaves and white of egg, and then put in the fire for some time. Probatum est.

Since Maspero is back here, everything in the museum is better regulated. According to him the new museum building is a beautiful piece of architecture but not practical, no expanse of walls and lots of bad lighting. Karnak is being re-erected in a solid manner, and new things are continually being found. I am convinced that the columns have fallen due to a light earthquake; they are very local and very frequent here.

I see you have of those coins. Do you want Egyptian ones? There are several thousands at my brother's, and here as well.

Probably there will be a lot of things for sale this summer, because Maspero wants to grant numerous permits for excavations. If you want something, I would like to know what would be most desirable: stelae, statues, small objects? To which amount? If I can secure a papyrus, should I buy it? You know that sometimes with such things it depends of a quick decision.

It is rather curious that inside the great enclosure of Karnak Phtah had a temple which was maintained by all dynasties and with the oldest stone. It is getting more and more probable that something predating the 11th will be found, and that the cult of Ammon was not recent but as ancient as the others. The map of Karnak should also be changed a lot, and many new details drawn in. If everything goes well, one may hope that in 10 years everything will be consolidated and much more will be visible.

With kind regards to the family and the gentlemen of the museum,
Sincerely yours,
J.H. Insinger
Luxor
11 March 1900

42. To Pleyte – RMO Archives 17.1.2/46: letters received 1900, no. 67

Dear Sir,

Today I cashed at the post office here 1 pound 22 piaster 1 millième = £E 1.221 and I return the receipt to you. The employee of the post made a mistake, though. 144 piaster = 1 pound 44 piaster or 1 pound 440 millièmes. The post office here reckons f 1.- the equivalent of 8,01 piaster.

---

35 William George Spencer Scott Compton, Marquess of Northampton (1851-1913), British nobleman who financed excavations in the Theban necropolis; see Bierbrier 2012, 129.
36 Édouard Naville (1844-1926), Swiss Egyptologist who excavated the mortuary temple of Queen Hatshepsut at Deir el-Bahari from 1893-1896, helped by the young artist Howard Carter who copied the wall reliefs. See Bierbrier 2012, 398-400 and 105-106.
37 James Edward Quibell (1867-1935), British Egyptologist who had a career with the Antiquities Service and in the Cairo Museum. See Bierbrier 2012, 450-451.
38 Émile Gaston Chassinat (1868-1948), French Egyptologist who succeeded Bouriant as director of the Institut Français (the 'mission') from 1898-1912. See Bierbrier 2012, 117-118.
39 This refers to Pleyte's daughter Petronella (born 1871), who would marry George Ignatz Witkowski from Berlin on 25 May 1899; see http://www.archiefleiden.nl/home/collecties/personen/zoek-op-personen/q/persoon_achternaam_t_0/%28pleyte%20OR%20pleijte%29/q/persoon_voornaam_t_0/petronella.
40 The reference is to the publication Morgan 1897, one of the first books about Egyptian prehistory.

8,01 /144,00\17,97, so f 17,97 and not f 15.88, as he reckoned; probably the man made the mistake to reckon with Turkish instead of Egyptian currency. We shall regard the f 2,09 as a modest gift to the museum.

I hear that a tomb has been found on the west bank, and one waits for Maspero to open it. This year 2600 + 800 + 180 pounds Egyptian will be given for the preservation of Karnak, perhaps even more; Legrain's work there is good, but they are now sending over engineers from Cairo who perhaps have no exact idea what to do under the circumstances.

I am too ill and weak to go out this winter, though recovering now, and then I hope to acquire something for the opened credit of f 500. For a couple of piasters I bought some flint implements which Legrain thought very beautiful (he is regarded here as something of an authority in this field). You can compare them then with the pre-Germanic ones. The Nile is so low that it reminds one of the Wilbour inscription.[41]

With kind regards,
Yours faithfully,
J.H. Insinger
Luxor
28 March 1900

43. To Pleyte – RMO Archives 17.1.2/46: letters received 1900, no. 173

Dear Sir,

Let me start by thanking you for sending the Catalogue by you and Mr Boeser.[42] I saw with great pleasure that some of the potsherds were worth describing. Since a while ago Professor Sayce and others were so frantically making purchases, that I thought Leyden should also have some. At first I was afraid I was flooding you, but yet I bought some more, most of them from Hermonthis (Erment) this time. I am sorry that I am not closer to Assuan, and have no contact there, for the best ones come from there.

Now I have a lot of prehistoric pots, a couple of figurines from Medinet, and 1 ushebti with 2 beautiful blue fragments of idem, + flint implements; one sizeable crate full. For the pots, I tried to find as many different varieties of size, shape, type of soil, and decoration as possible, and I possess most types listed by de Morgan in his Origines.[43] (There was a gold mounted flint knife, but it was sold for £ 50.- before I heard about it). Prices will not disappoint you, for I bought most pots assorted for 10 piaster, ± f 1.25. On top of that a ceramic house for f 10.-, four towers with 2 floors each surrounded by a wall and with figurines inside (originally from Gebelein), that I attribute to the time of the Xth. I wrote to the consulate whether I could send it there to be sealed at the museum, but received no answer. Our ignoble consular system should be utterly changed or else abolished. Those people do <u>nothing</u>.

When those people behave conceitedly, may I then include a small box of coins in the shipment that is <u>not</u> destined for the museum (you did not care about them) but for a cousin? Costs of transport and customs for my account according to the weight.

I waited so long because I wanted to have a pot with ships; finally I found one which includes the flags (see de Morgan) plus one with mountains and ostriches

and … below I believe .. a marque de fabrique (14 pots large and small altogether for f 10.-).

If your publications continue at the same rate, my name will be better known than yours or that of Mr Boeser.

This morning a beautiful piece of shroud was offered for sale to me, with two cartouches, exactly like those we took from the Ramesside group;[44] colour of the ink the real brownish red, but … not genuine. What do these fellows imagine; this winter an Englishman will probably spend about ten pounds for it.

My kindest regards to your family (the Mr Pleyte who worked so hard at the exhibition must be your son?)[45], to Mr Boeser and the other gentlemen of the museum.

Yours faithfully,
J.H. Insinger
Luxor
14 Aug 1900
It might be useful to write immediately to the ministry in order to speed up matters.

---

41 Wilbour was the first to copy the famous Famine Inscription on the island of Sehel; see http://www.brooklynmuseum.org/community/blogosphere/2010/06/24/wilbour-and-the-stela-of-the-seven-years-famine-part-i/.

42 I.e. the catalogue on Coptic objects, which contains some of the ostraca bought from Insinger (Pleyte/Boeser 1900).

43 See note 40 above.

44 I.e. the royal cachette of Deir el Bahari.

45 This refers to Cornelis Marinus Pleyte (1863-1917), son of Willem Pleyte and himself a museum curator and specialist of Indonesia. In 1900 he was involved in the organisation and display of the colonial exhibition at the Dutch pavilion of the World Exhibition in Paris. See http://en.wikipedia.org/wiki/Cornelis_Marinus_Pleyte.

44. To Pleyte – RMO Archives 17.1.2/46: letters received 1900, no. 177

Dear Sir,

The Consulate at Cairo declared they were prepared to take care of the shipment, so that it will soon take place.

Sincerely,
J.H. Insinger
Luxor
18 Aug 1900

45. To Pleyte – RMO Archives 17.1.2/46: letters received 1900, no. 184

Dear Sir,

Yesterday I sent a crate to the deputy Consul in Cairo, with the request to have it sealed at the Gizeh museum in order to enable it to pass the customs, and to take care of the further shipment. Enclosed you will find a description of the contents and the costs made so far. The packing was done with cotton and hacked straw, so that I hope no accidents will happen. I intended to have it insured at the railway station here, but the officials stated they are not allowed to insure fragile goods.

The findspot of most things is Gebeleen, unless stated otherwise. The 231 tesserae[46] Karnak, the others Erment. This is always according to what the dealers say, who tell terrific lies sometimes.

Though I was in doubt whether the decoration of two pots was genuine, as I did not remember to have seen something similar before, and that decoration displays some similarity to Arabic characters, I thought I had to send them, also because they were in the same lot as the important ostrich vase. Illustrations of most of them are to be found in de Morgan, Origines de l'Egypte.

I believe the 4 ceramic statuettes from Medinet Habou represent a type not yet present in Leyden, however unattractive they may be as such. With all respect,

Yours faithfully,
J.H. Insinger
Luxor
31 Aug 1900

46. To Pleyte – RMO Archives 17.1.2/46: letters received 1900, no. 198

Dear Mr Pleyte!

I hope the shipment will please you as much as your letter pleased me. I am still collecting pots, for myself in fact, but if you want more I can help you. I also ordered some fellows to buy glass beads; c'est tout la rage. There are some with decidedly Arabic motifs, others like one makes them today in Venice (from Egypt or Italy, made where originally?), and others very clearly Pharaonic. Murch[47] bought fine ones for the Brittish museum. And I continue looking for papyri; however, the supervision has improved a little, and there are fewer excavations.

Meanwhile, I believe it would not be untimely if you wrote to the minister that a couple of catalogue numbers came to Leyden thanks to my intervention. Over the years, I also sent quite a lot to other museums (Ethnographical, e.g.); I am rather the most prominent Dutchman in Egypt, and <u>yet I have unpleasant experiences with our Consul General</u>. Many people had thought that on the occasion of 31 Aug 1898 my name would occur on the great list,[48] and if H.E. wants to send me a decoration with the feast of St Nicholas he would not do a bad job. (I would rather have nothing to do with his medals).

Professor Sayce published something about prehistoric, or at least pre-pharaonic cylinders at the time.[49] There were 6 known to him, 2 of which belong to me, and I am sending you an impression. Also an impression of something which is either a gnostic monstrosity, or … the primeval scarab. I showed it to many people, among others to Sayce, Legrain, and the antiquities dealers; nobody had ever seen something similar; the dealers were unanimous in stating that nobody in Egypt ever made such kind of things, and that it must be genuine; and I bought the item, which is made of the same kind of black stone as the cylinders which are pharaonic beyond all doubt, <u>together with</u> one of the cylinders from a man who had prehistoric junk.

Regarding the decoration of some of the pots about which I had my doubts, the following: I later bought a pot of the same clay with

---

46   Ostraca.

47   Chauncey Murch (1856-1907), American missionary and collector, who negotiated the British Museum's payments for many objects obtained by Budge; see Bierbrier 2012, 392.

48   See above, n. 32. The remark about St Nicholas is a joke: on the eve of that saint's feast (5 December) the Dutch are in the habit of giving each other presents, pretending they come from the saint.

49   See Sayce 1900. This article does not mention any cylinders in Insinger's collection. Unfortunately, the lacquer impressions cannot be found nowadays.

What I did with the brush, the maker had done with his finger; a successor did it with a stick or swab of textile, yet another took a finer split stick; the ductus is the natural one if the pot is held in the left hand and is touched with a right finger, and I am starting to believe that this decoration on your pots represents a natural development of mine, which is older.

With kind regards, also to Mr Boeser and the family,
Yours faithfully,
J.H. Insinger
Luxor
21 Sept 1900
The impressions in lacquer will come as registered mail, as samples without value

47. To Pleyte – RMO Archives 17.1.2/46: letters received 1900, no. 240

Dear Mr Pleyte!

Because I had to go to Cairo in order to consult the doctor, of course I also went to the museum, and to my surprise found out that the crate had not been delivered until October 7th in order to be sealed. My box of coins had been shipped one month before by the kind offices of the banker! Of course the people who are now working at the museum would never cause trouble for a shipment to somebody like you by somebody like me, and I had written so to the consulate. However, it seems that laziness is like a contamination affecting our consulates.

Meanwhile, I have continued buying pots, and have a rather complete collection. If you want some more now, I shall send them, otherwise I shall construct a couple of showcases around them and keep them for myself. Likewise, I bought quite a few flints, including some fine ones, but in order to get them I had to take many ordinary scrapers or scratchers into the bargain. It may be very nice to collect, etc., but one feels sad thinking of all that is irreparably lost due to the robbing and digging by the natives.

At the time, probably while you were travelling, I wrote you that Mr G. Legrain, whose advice I asked at the time about the papyrus, told me he had photographed the first part (which is exactly the missing one) at the time, and that he was quite prepared to put it at your disposal but also would like to receive a copy of your publication. It is so rare that one is able to publish a complete papyrus, even though one does not have the whole thing in one's possession, and the purchase and publication have already cost such a lot, that I take the liberty to strongly advise you to spend the extra tenner, and print the beginning separately on loose pages which can then be bound together with the rest.

Legrain's address is: Luxor, Egypt (inspecteur-dessinateur du service des antiquités). He is again busily working at Karnak. The weak columns are laid out on the ground course by course, the foundations are renewed, fragments fallen down are re-inserted in their place; the pylon between hypostyle hall and Bubastide court, of which the west side has collapsed and which stands so unstable that it endangers the hypostyle hall, probably has to be dismantled stone by stone and then re-erected; likewise the obelisks which lie to the ground in pieces, and all the time something new and unexpected comes up.

S.v.p. kind regards to your family and Mr Boeser; my wife sometimes asks me whether Mr Pleyte will ever come to Egypt after all this writing.

Yours faithfully,
J.H. Insinger
Luxor
31 Oct 1900

48. RMO Archives 19.7.2/1: archives Pleyte, correspondence

[excerpt from letter of J.H. Insinger dated 30 Dec. 1900[50])

The c's[51] are doubtless genuine, one of them has been published by Sayce. I bought the scar. together with the 1st cyl. from a man who had a lot of prehist. stuff: bone combs, hair pins, etc. etc. Maspero, Sayce, Bourriant, Daressy, Legrain, Murch, the native dealers all agreed that they had never seen anything like it, but therefore did not dare to doubt the authenticity. The antiquities dealers told me that there was nobody who could produce such craftsmanship. All this is at least 10 years ago, I think. Only now do forged cylinders appear on the market, but one recognizes them instantly. On the whole I believe Sayce published 9 of them. There will not have been found much more than 20 ...

Yesterday Sweinfurth and Herold passed by. I showed them cyl. and scar., full of admiration for the latter.

---

50 Possibly this date has to be read as 1908, the year when Insinger again discussed the matter of the seals. However, since the letter was found in the Pleyte archive and Pleyte died in 1903, this would mean the document has been filed in the wrong place. The handwriting rather looks like that of Pleyte himself.

51 I.e. cylinder seals.

49. To Pleyte – RMO Archives 17.1.2/47: letters received 1901, no. 14

Dear Sir!

Yesterday your letter arrived with remittance to the Crédit Lyonnais of f 123,15. I really do not know anymore how much I stated to you in Piasters. 8 piasters is almost = f 1.-. I hope it will be alright.

Of course it pleased me immensely that you seem to like the whole lot. I did not hear any complaints about breakage, and accordingly think I may hope that the packing was sufficient. In the meantime I again bought pots and flints, also a few items of ivory, rather with the idea to form a collection of those things myself, but I shall now pack them also again. Leyden will then have a collection of all types and varieties mentioned by de Morgan, except for red pots on legs with black collar, and white-figured ones. Of the latter kind I only saw one, and the decoration looked very suspicious to me then. On the other hand, there are several types which are not mentioned by de Morgan.

I can also get some Demotic papyri; Capart told me they were very good as far as he could judge. If they have not gone by the time your answer arrives, should I buy them?

There are Coptic sheets of parchment for sale, belonging to the collection which I sent you in the past, and which were published together with the book of Anastasiadis.[52] But the fellow asks twenty pounds for an Albert biscuit tin full (and not even chock-full). I now ask all scholars not too buy them, and hope to get them next spring. Do you want them? For how much?

Capart was here, and I tried to help him; I succeeded in getting him a book of the dead with nice illustrations: he wanted to have une pièce d'étalage; but the owner asked £ 70, and within five minutes Capart got it for £ 35,-. He was too much taken by it and found it too pretty; but he did not want to wait until the next day, being afraid of Budge and Schiaparelli.[53] Otherwise he could have had the thing for £ 25.- à £ 30.-.[54]

The falsifications are worse than ever this year. Even the most honest (?) dealers are involved, and the most clever ones are also cheated by them. One of the biggest dealers here, Abdel megid Hasseen,[55] has fallen into the trap for ± £ 560.-!!

Therefore Capart, Legrain, and the others often disagree; everybody tells the other: have you bought another piece of trash again? The best authority, as always, is Maspero with his myopic eyes. After half an hour he concluded that a head bought by Capart was probably genuine, and dated to the XIIIrd, but that others probably would regard it as a forgery!

I feel very sorry because of what you write about your health. Here we have a young Dutchman, van Stolk from Rotterdam, for his 4th winter, who used to suffer from his bladder and kidneys; now he has almost recovered. I heartily wish you all the best, and such health that you may still feel appetite one day to see the Pyramids and Karnak with your own eyes. It is about time, for one of these days yet another large portion of the ceiling of the hall of gold in the tomb of Sethi I came down.

Karnak continues to be interesting, and produced two statues of Usortesen II,[56] plus an important stela about Queen Ahmosis, who played a major part in the expulsion of the Hyksos according to what her son writes.[57]

With kind regards to the family members and Mr Boeser,

Yours faithfully,
J.H. Insinger
Luxor
19 Jan 1901

50. To Pleyte – RMO Archives 17.1.2/47: letters received 1901, no. 135

Dear Mr Pleyte,

Today I am sending you three crates again, for which I send you a table of contents hereby. It contains some items which were highly valued by the Egyptologists passing here. It includes several types not illustrated by de Morgan. Especially the conical pots were appreciated.

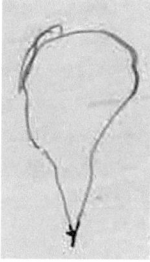

---

52. For 'Anastasy'. The book in question is a Coptic codex (inv. AMS 9), which together with the Insinger manuscripts makes up the bulk of the publication (Pleyte/Boeser 1897).
53. Ernesto Schiaparelli (1856-1928), Italian Egyptologist, director of the Turin Museum from 1894-1927 who undertook excavations from 1903 onwards but before that spent some time in Egypt making purchases. See Bierbrier 2012, 492-493.
54. Doubtless this concerns the famous Book of the Dead papyrus of Neferrenpet, bought by Capart at Luxor in the winter of 1900-1901. See Van de Walle/Limme/De Meulenaere 1980, 22 with n. 47.
55. See Hagen/Ryholt 2016, 184-185, where he is said to be the brother-in-law of Mohammed Mohassib. Capart bought the Neferrenpet papyrus from this very same dealer (see the previous footnote).
56. See above, n. 15.
57. This is the Karnak stela of Ahmose; see Legrain 1903, 27-29; Breasted 1906, § 29-32.

I could not obtain much in the way of finely worked flints. Competition is enormous. At first I wished to keep the pots for myself, but your last letter demonstrated so much satisfaction about the shipment, that I decided to send the stuff on. Cairo of course has a complete set. By travelling to and fro and digging himself, Schiaparelli managed to secure many things I could not get, but even so I believe that Leyden does not cut a bad figure as far as prehistory is concerned.

I shall be travelling this month, to Italy. I have some faint hope to secure a couple of papyri before I leave, though this should be read with a question mark.

Many of the tesserae come from the tax office at Karnak, which Legrain found just to the North of the length of quay where he discovered the interesting Nile levels.

Antiquities are getting rare and <u>very</u> expensive; colossal demand, lesser production. Falsifications are therefore remarkably good. The well-known dealer Abdel megied Hasseen fell into the trap for £ 550.-!! I hope you will conclude that I did not buy to expensively.

With all respect, and kind regards to family and museum,
Yours faithfully,
J.H. Insinger
Luxor
1 June 1901

I send a few items as presents which I myself received in order to thank me.

[enclosed table of contents, 6 pages]

There are numbers and prices inside the pots and packages in order to ease the identification. I am already dreading the curses of Mr Boeser who has to empty the crates, clean the contents, join the pieces together, provide the labels, and draw up the catalogue. I hope everything will arrive in good order. If the money is remitted before Oct. 1st, please send it for me to Ludwig Müller, banker, Cairo.

J.H.I.

51. To Pleyte – RMO Archives 17.1.2/47: letters received 1901, no. 193

Dear Mr Pleyte,

I have to answer two letters, one of 29 July from Mr Boeser, the other of 14 Aug from you which arrived here today. I heard from my daughter about the operation to your foot, and from Mr Boeser fortunately that you were doing so well. Of course I am pleased that you like the shipment. Naturally, buying such things is always a bit of a question, because after a <u>single</u> superficial visit to Leiden I know so badly what is missing, what is most desired, so I may count myself lucky that both you and Mr Boeser seem to be happy. Regarding the oldest pots, I think Leiden will not cut a bad figure now when compared to other museums, and all is well if also the prices are not too disappointing. For also in that respect I have no idea whether I stroke a good or a bad bargain, and would appreciate some directions if the occasion arises. If you could let me know which object seemed to be extra expensive or extra cheap to you, accompanied by a small description of the item (I do not know all these things by heart), then I would no longer buy too expensively in the future. One lives and learns!

I intend to take ship in Venice on the 5th, and to return to Luxor by the 21st. By then there are rarely any buyers and tourists around, and occasionally one may strike a good bargain, but the cream has by long been taken from the milk; there are fewer excavations than there used to be, and that man Budge for instance also sometimes comes in Oct., and pays far too much. If upon arrival I find instructions how much I can spend approximately, and on what things, then I could of course again send you something. <u>Papyri are expensive</u>, I am not an expert, there is not always somebody around whom I can consult, such as Legrain for the great Leiden papyrus. If there are any, I shall buy them with pleasure, but without taking any responsibility.

I hope to hear by then that you will have had a complete recovery. The hope of seeing you sometime in Egypt becomes fainter and fainter, and it is improbable I shall be coming to the Netherlands once more. With kind regards also to the ladies,

All yours,
J.H. Insinger
Pallanza
28 Aug 1901

52. To Pleyte – RMO Archives 17.1.2/47: letters received 1901, no. 213

Dear Mr Pleyte,

As a consequence of my travels the letters have been roaming about a bit. For instance your n° 185 d.d. 29 Aug. which I did not receive until a few days ago. The signed receipt goes enclosed hereby. Müller in Cairo told me he had also cashed already. I am pleased that in general the junk was to your liking. For the first coming days now I have a lot to do in the house, and I did not see a dealer yet, but I shall remember your instructions regarding small items. If I happen to see a sizeable object which I think worthwhile, then I shall try to purchase that too. Last year I just saw 2 examples of black pots with white lines, and those seemed suspicious to me, so I did not buy any. Last winter a prehist. mummy in contracted position, perfectly preserved but without bitumen, was bought for Turin.[58] Should I be able to acquire something similar, I shall also spend a large sum if necessary.

It is now humid and warm here, no wind, so oppressive; after Europe one feels it doubly.

With best wishes for a continuous good health, and kind regards to your family and Dr Boeser, I remain with all respect,

Yours faithfully,
J.H. Insinger
Luxor
21 Sept 1901

53. To Boeser – RMO Archives 17.2.1/6: letters received 1906-1923, He-Jy

Dear Sir!

I received the enclosed letter from Mr Chassinat, and then "De monumenten van het Oude Rijk" of Leyden,[59] with the attached label: Musée d'Antiquités des Pays-Bas, and my address.

May I politely ask you for information? Is it the French Ministry of Education or the Leyden museum which is sending me this atlas?

With best thanks in advance,
Yours faithfully,
J.H. Insinger
Luxor
21 June 1908

54. To Holwerda – RMO Archives 17.2.1/6: ontvangen brieven 1906-1923, He-Jy

Dear Sir!

In possession of your honoured [letter] n° 321 d.d. 29 June, I have the honour hereby to express my thanks for the dispatch of: Monumenten van het Oude Rijk. I hope you will manage to obtain my receipt for this publication from the French government, which I had to send to Mr Casanova.

I use the opportunity to draw your attention to the fact that objects from Gebel-ein of a different make than the former ones are offered for sale to me. Apparently a large prehistoric cemetery there is being plundered and destroyed by natives. I think I have to point out to you that the greatest heat is over; most work is now suspended, so that in this time of year one can get workmen cheaply. The prices of boats have dropped a lot, and it will be rare for such a good opportunity to present itself for scientifically exploring this site for that period. Of course one would need to apply for an excavation permit.

With all respect,
Yours faithfully,
J.H. Insinger
Luxor
12 July 1908

55. To Boeser – RMO Archives 17.2.1/6: letters received 1906-1923, He-Jy

Dear Sir!

Some time ago a doctor from Sloterdijk-Zaandam wrote me regarding the Racial Portraits by Petrie.[60] However, the gentleman's signature is so unclear that I cannot decipher it, and the envelope on which it was legible has been torn up. May I politely request you to inform the gentleman that Petrie writes me the following addition: the photos have not been published but can be printed on demand. Orders should be sent to Mr Murray, 34 Dartmouth Park Hill, London N.W. Further publications were not made on the subject by P.

Concerning the cylinders:[61] Professor Sayce was here some time ago. Most of them have been published by him, among them one of mine. He says that the price varies from £ 1.- to £ 10.- per item, and that mine certainly belong to the best ones. I asked the dealers here about a

---

58 This is Turin no. S.293, a mummy provided with various burial gifts bought by Schiaparelli in the winter of 1900-1901. See Vassilika 2009, 7.
59 Holwerda/Boeser/Holwerda 1905, sent because the first two plates depict prehistoric pottery bought from Insinger. Unfortunately, Boeser's answers to Insinger's letters do not seem to have been preserved in the RMO archives.
60 For this publication, see Petrie 1887. For a recent discussion, see Sheppard 2010.
61 *Cf.* above, letters nos. **46** and **48**.

price, and the answer was: "they are so rare that you have to pay fancy prices". The sum offered therefore seems to me far too low.

Sayce remembered very well to have seen the scarab here, and called it: "that most wonderful stone". Unless the Leyden museum makes a much higher bid, therefore, I am not inclined to hand over my stones to that institution.

I am very sorry that none of the gentlemen from Leyden comes here for the archaeological congress.[62] Apparently it will be very well attended, though there are also numerous archaeophiles among the participants.

With all respect,
Yours faithfully,
J.H. Insinger
Luxor
7 April 1909

56. To Boeser – RMO Archives 17.2.1/6: letters received 1906-1923, He-Jy

Dear Sir!

In an Egyptian newspaper (which I hope to be able to send to you) there is a report that Seymour de Ricci[63] would have purchased fragments of the Suten Xeft; that he and Spiegelberg partly deciphered it, and that Noël Giron would have proved these are parts of the missing beginning.[64] Frenay told me at the time that he sent the papyrus intact to the Louvre, and that Revillout (though acquainted with the conditions of the agreement) partly opened it in an inadvertent manner and broke it, and ... made a partial copy even so.

In that case the Ricci fragments would belong to another copy.

With all respect,
Yours faithfully,
J.H. Insinger
Luxor
13 April 1909

---

62 This congress was organised in Alexandria and Cairo from April 7 to 14, 1909 and had 860 participants; see Ransom 1909.

63 Seymour Montefiore Robert Rosso de Ricci (1881-1942), British bibliographer and antiquary who owned several important papyri, including parts of the Insinger papyrus (published under the name Suten Xeft by Pleyte/Boeser 1899) which are now in the Collège de France in Paris, Fonds Seymour de Ricci, Objet 193-200. See Bierbrier 2012, 464-465 and cf. http://www.trismegistos.org/daht/detail.php?tm=55918.

64 Noël Aimé-Giron (1884-1941), French orientalist; see Bierbrier 2012, 9. For the publication in question, see Aimé-Giron 1908.

Abbreviations

ASAE	Annales du Service d'Antiquités de l'Égypte
BdE	Bibliothèque d'Étude
BHA	Bulletin for the History of Archaeology
BIE	Bulletin de l'Institut Égyptien
CGC	Catalogue général des antiquités égyptiennes du Musée du Caire
CNMAL	Collections of the National Museum of Antiquities at Leiden
CRAIBL	Comptes Rendues de l'Académie des Inscriptions et de Belles Lettres
LÄ	Lexikon der Ägyptologie (eds. W. Helck/W. Westendorf), Wiesbaden
MMAF	Mémoires publiés par les membres de la mission archéologique française au Caire
OMRO	Oudheidkundige Mededelingen uit het Rijksmuseum van Oudheden te Leiden
PSBA	Proceedings of the Society of Biblical Archaeology
RdE	Revue d'Égyptologie

Bibliography

Aimé-Giron, N., 1908: Nouvelles maximes en démotique appartenant au papyrus moral de Leyde, CRAIBL 1908, 29-36.

Atiya, A.S. (ed.), 1991: The Coptic Encyclopedia, 1-8, New York/Toronto.

Baedeker, K., 1891: Ägypten, Handbuch für Reisende, II: Ober-Ägypten und Nubien bis zum Zweiten Katarakt, Leipzig.

Baedeker, K., 1898: Égypte, manuel de voyage, Leipzig.

Bagnall, R.S./Sijpesteijn, P.J./Worp, K.A., 1980: Greek ostraca, a catalogue of the collection of Greek ostraca in the National Museum of Antiquities at Leiden with a chapter on the Greek ostraca in the Papyrological Institute of the University of Leiden, CNMAL 4, Zutphen.

Bierbrier, M.L., 2012: Who was who in Egyptology, London.

Bissing, F.W. von, 1955: Ägyptische Lebensweisheit, Zurich.

Boeser, P.A.A., 1920: Transkription und Übersetzung des Papyrus Insinger, OMRO 3.1.

Bothmer, B.V., 1974: Numbering systems of the Cairo Museum, in: Textes et languages de l'Égypte pharaonique, BdE 64/3, 111-122.

Breasted, J.H., 1906: Ancient records of Egypt, II, Chicago.

Bresciani, E., 1969: Letteratura e poesia dell' antico Egitto, Turin.

Brunner, H., 1988: Altägyptische Weisheit, Zurich/Munich.

Budge, E.A. Wallis, 1920: By Nile and Tigris, a narrative of journeys to Egypt and Mesopotamia on behalf of the British Museum between the years 1886 and 1913, I-II, London.

Capart, J., 1936: Travels in Egypt (Dec., 1880, to May, 1891), letters of Charles Edwin Wilbour, Brooklyn.

Carstens, P.R., 2014: The encyclopedia of Egypt during the reign of the Mehemet Ali dynasty (1798-1952), Victoria BC.

Daressy, G., 1922: Un casse-tête préhistorique de Gébelein, ASAE 22, 17-32.

Desroches-Noblecourt, C./Vercoutter, J. (eds.), 1981: Un siècle de fouilles françaises en Égypte, 1880-1980, Paris.

Dümichen, J., 1865-1866: Geographische Inschriften altägyptischer Denkmäler, Leipzig.

Edwards, A.B., 1878: A thousand miles up the Nile, Leipzig.

Erman, A., 1929: Mein Werden und mein Werken, Erinnerungen eines alten berliner Gelehrten, Leipzig.

Esteva, X.D, 2016: Viatges per Egipte d'Eduard Toda i Güell 1884-1886, II, [n.pl.].

Fiechter, J.J., 2005: Faux et faussaires en art égyptien, Turnhout.

Gaillard, C./Daressy, G., 1905: La faune momifiée de l'antique Égypte, CGC, Cairo.

Gessler-Löhr, B., 1997: Bemerkungen zur Nekropole des Neuen Reiches von Saqqara vor der Amarna-Zeit, II: Gräber der Bürgermeister von Memphis, OMRO 77, 31-71.

Hagen, F./Ryholt, K., 2016: The antiquities trade in Egypt 1880-1930, the H.O. Lange papers, Copenhagen.

Halbertsma, R.B., 1995: Le solitaire des ruïnes: de archeologische reizen van Jean Emile Humbert (1771-1839) in dienst van het Koninkrijk der Nederlanden, CNMAL 9, Leiden.

Halbertsma, R.B., 2003: Scholars, travellers and trade: the pioneer years of the National Museum of Antiquities in Leiden, 1818-1840, London/New York.

Hasselbach, H., 1987: Bibliografie van W. Pleyte, OMRO 67, 93-99.

Henein, N.H., 1988: Mārī Girgis: village de Haute-Égypte, Cairo.

Holwerda, A.E.J., 1905: Monumens égyptiens du Musée d'Antiquités des Pays-Bas à Leide, 34 supplement: Suten-xeft, le livre royal, Leiden.

Holwerda, A.E.J./Boeser, P.A.A./Holwerda, J.H., 1905: Beschrijving van de Egyptische verzameling in het Rijksmuseum van Oudheden in Leiden, I: De monumenten van het Oude Rijk, The Hague.

Hooft, Ph.P.M. van 't/Raven, M.J./Rooij, E.H.C. van/Vogelsang-Eastwood, G.M., 1994: Pharaonic and early medieval Egyptian textiles, CNMAL 8, Leiden.

Hyvernat, H., 1933: Introduction to E. Porcher, Analyse des manuscrits coptes 131^{1-8} de la Bibliothèque Nationale, avec indication des textes bibliques, RdE 1, 105-116.

Insinger, J.H., 1885: In het land der Nijl-cataracten, Februari-Maart 1883, Tijdschrift van het Aardrijkskundig Genootschap, IInd series, vol. 2, 1-113.

Insinger, J.H./(Raven, M.J., ed.), 2004: In het land der Nijlcataracten (1883), Leuven/Leiden.

Ismail, M., 2011: Wallis Budge, magic and mummies in London and Cairo, Glasgow.

James, T.G.H., 1981: The British Museum and Ancient Egypt, London.
James, T.G.H. (ed.), 1982: Excavating in Egypt, the Egypt Exploration Society, 1882-1982, London.
James, T.G.H., 1992: Howard Carter, the path to Tutankhamun, London/New York.
Kanawati, N., 1980: The rock tombs of el-Hawawish, the cemetery of Akhmim, I, Sydney.
Keurs, P. ter/Wirtz, W. (eds.), 2018: Rijksmuseum van Oudheden Leiden, een geschiedenis van 200 jaar, Leiden/Zwolle.
Khater, A., 1960: Le régime juridique des fouilles et des antiquités en Égypte, Cairo.
Kitchen, K.A., 1973: The Third Intermediate Period in Egypt (1100-650 BC), Warminster.
Legrain, G., 1903: Second rapport sur les travaux exécutés à Karnak du 31 octobre 1901 au 15 mai 1902, ASAE 4, 1-40.
Lepsius, K.R., 1849-1859: Denkmäler aus Aegypten und Aethiopien, Berlin.
Lichtheim, M., 1980: Ancient Egyptian literature, a book of readings, III: the Late Period, London.
Mahmoud, A., 2011: Catalogue of funerary objects from the tomb of the servant in the place of truth Sennedjem, Cairo.
Maspero, G., 1884: Voyage d'inspection en 1884, BIE IIe ser. 5, 62-71.
Maspero, G., 1886: Fouilles exécutées en Égypte de 1881 à 1885, BIE IIe ser. 6, 3-91.
Maspero, G., 1887a: L'archéologie égyptienne, Paris.
Maspero, G., 1887b: Rapport à l'Institut Égyptien sur les fouilles et travaux exécutés en Égypte pendant l'hiver de 1885-1886, BIE IIe ser. 7, 196-271.
Maspero, G., 1889a: Trois années de fouilles dans les tombeaux de Thèbes et de Memphis, MMAF 1, Cairo, 133-242.
Maspero, G., 1889b: Les momies royales de Déir el-Baharî, MMAF 1, Cairo, 511-787.
Maspero, G., 1892: Fragments de manuscrits coptes-thébains provenant de la bibliothèque du Deir-Amba-Shenoudah, MMAF 6.1, Paris.
Maspero, G., 1895-1897: Histoire ancienne des peuples de l'Orient classique, I-II, Paris.
Maspero, G., 1901: Sur l'existence d'un temple mystérieux dans le désert à l'ouest du Saîd, ASAE 2, 146-153.
Morgan, J. de, 1896: Compte rendu des travaux archéologiques effectués par le Service des Antiquités de l'Égypte et par les savants étrangers pendant les années 1894-1895, BIE IIIe ser. 6, 107-154.
Morgan, J. de, 1897: Recherches sur les origines de l'Égypte: ethnographie préhistorique et tombeau royal de Négadah, Paris.

Nederland's Patriciaat 1988: Nederland's Patriciaat, genealogieën van bekende geslachten, vol. 72, The Hague.
Nur el-Din, M.A.A., 1974: The demotic ostraca in the National Museum of Antiquities at Leiden, CNMAL 1, Leiden.
Perez, N.N., 1988: Focus East, early photography in the Near East (1839-1885), New York/Jerusalem.
Petrie, W.M.F., 1887: Racial photographs from the Egyptian monuments, London.
Petrie, W.M.F., 1931: Seventy years in archaeology, London.
Pleyte, W./Boeser, P.A.A., 1897: Manuscrits coptes du Musée d'Antiquités des Pays-Bas à Leide, publiés d'après les ordres du gouvernement, Leiden.
Pleyte, W./Boeser, P.A.A., 1899: Monumens égyptiens du Musée d'Antiquités des Pays-Bas à Leide, 34: Suten-xeft, le livre royal: papyrus démotique Insinger, Leiden.
Pleyte, W./Boeser, P.A.A., 1900: Catalogue du Musée d'Antiquités à Leide, sous-division F. Égypte: Antiquités coptes, Leiden.
Porter, B./Moss, R.L.B., 1937: Topographical bibliography of Ancient Egyptian hieroglyphic texts, reliefs and paintings, V: Upper Egypt, sites, Oxford.
Porter, B./Moss, R.L.B., 1974: Topographical bibliography of Ancient Egyptian hieroglyphic texts, reliefs, and paintings, III^2/1: Memphis, Abû Rawâsh to Abûsîr, Oxford.
Quibell, J.E., 1901: Flint dagger from Gebelein, ASAE 2, 131-132.
Ransom, C.L., 1909: The International Congress of Archaeologists, Classical Philology 4.3, 311-313.
Raven, M.J., 1991: Insinger and early photography in Egypt, OMRO 71, 13-27.
Raven, M.J., 1993: Mummies onder het mes, Amsterdam.
Raven, M.J./Taconis, W.K., 2005: Egyptian mummies, radiological atlas of the collections in the National Museum of Antiquities at Leiden, Turnhout.
Raven, M.J., 2007: Hakken in het zand, 50 jaar opgraven in Egypte door het Rijksmuseum van Oudheden, Leiden.
Raven, M.J., 2009: Insinger in el-Kab, in: Claes, W./Meulenaere, H. De/Hendrickx, S. (eds.), Elkab and beyond, Studies in honour of Luc Limme, Leuven, 195-212.
Reeves, C.N., 1990: Valley of the Kings, the decline of a royal necropolis, London/New York.
Reeves, N./Wilkinson, R.H., 1996: The complete Valley of the Kings, tombs and treasures of Egypt's greatest Pharaohs, London.
Reid, D.M., 2002: Whose Pharaohs? Archaeology, museums, and Egyptian national identity from

Napoleon to World War I, Berkeley/Los Angeles/London.

Ritner, R.K., 2009: The Libyan anarchy: inscriptions from Egypt's Third Intermediate Period, Atlanta.

Sayce, A.H., 1900: (I) Objects from the tomb of a prædynastic Egyptian king. (II) Some early Egyptian seal-cylinders, PSBA 22, 278-280.

Sayce, A.H., 1923: Reminiscences, London.

Schiaparelli, E., 1921: La missione italiana a Ghebelein, ASAE 21, 126-128.

Schneider, H.D., 1977: Shabtis, an introduction to the history of Ancient Egyptian funerary statuettes, with a catalogue of the collections of shabtis in the National Museum of Antiquities at Leiden, I-III, CNMAL 2, Leiden.

Sheppard, K.L., 2010: Flinders Petrie and eugenics at UCL, BHA 20(1), 16-29 (= http://dx.doi.org/10.5334/bha.2013).

Smith, G. Elliott, 1912: The royal mummies, CGC, Cairo.

Steindorff, G., 1901: Grabfunde des Mittleren Reiches in den Königlichen Museen zu Berlin, II: Der Sarg des Sebk-o. Ein Grabfund aus Gebelên, Berlin.

Stenvert, R., *et al.*, 2004: Monumenten in Nederland: Zuid-Holland, Zeist/Zwolle.

Thompson, J., 2015: Wonderful things, a history of egyptology, 2: the golden age: 1881-1914, Cairo/New York.

Toda, E., 1920: La découverte et l'inventaire du tombeau de Sen-nezem, ASAE 20, 145-158.

Vassilika, E., 2009: I capolavori del Museo Egizio di Torino, Turin/Florence.

Walle, B. Van de/Limme, L./Meulenaere, H. De, 1980: Musées Royaux d'Art et d'Histoire, la collection égyptienne, les étapes marquantes de son développement, Brussels.

Wijngaarden, W.D. van, 1931: Een kistje voor sperwermummies, OMRO 12, 1-4.

Wijngaarden, W.D. van, 1933: Uit de collectie Insinger, OMRO 14, 1-4.

Wijngaarden, W.D. van, 1935: Van Heurnius tot Boeser, drie eeuwen Egyptologie in Nederland (1620-1935), Leiden.

Wilkinson, J.G., 1858: Handbook for travellers in Egypt, London.

Wilson, J.A., 1964: Signs & wonders upon Pharaoh, Chicago/London.

Indices

1. Persons, modern

Abbas II, Khedive 20-21
Abd-el-Megid Hussein 80-81
Abd-er-Rasul 16
Amélineau 29
Anastasy 75, 80
Anslijn 13, 21
Boeser 20, 29, 36, 42, 55-56, 73, 75, 77, 79-83
Borchardt 71
Bouriant 16, 19, 26, 62, 64, 76, 79
Bretschneider 73, 75
Brugsch 16-17, 26, 54, 61-62
Budge 21, 53-55, 58, 80-81
Capart 15, 21, 80
Carter 21-22, 54, 58, 76
Casanova 82
Chassinat 76, 82
Cromer, Lord 20
Daraoun
- M. 14, 16, 21-22, 70, 79
- Y. 15, 19
Daressy 73, 76, 79
Dawson 49
Does de Willebois, van der 21, 36, 53, 64, 68-70, 73
Edwards 12-13
Emma, Queen 75
Erman 29, 65
Fischer 25
Franz I, Emperor 62
Frénay 29, 31, 35-36, 50-52, 68-69, 83
Gayet 16
Giron 83
Grébaut 16, 19, 32, 34-35, 53, 55-56, 64, 66
Grenfell 63
Heemskerk 30-31, 53, 63
Herold 79
Héron 13
Holwerda
- A.E.J. 20, 43, 82
- J.H. 43-44
Humbert 8
Hussein Kamel, Sultan 18, 21
Insinger
- E.H.D. 14, 19, 21-22, 47

- F. 15
- F.J. 14
- F.M.H. 14-16, 20-21, 57
- H.A. 11, 16, 18, 20-21
- J.H.O. 47
- O.C.H. 14, 70
- W.A. 29, 32, 37, 43-44, 50, 61-62, 64-66, 70-71, 75-76
Insinger-Everwijn Lange 44, 47
Ismail, Khedive 12, 18, 35, 52
Iversen 21-22
Kitchener 72
Klasens 54
Kurtas 67
Ledid 29, 32, 44
Leemans 7-8, 17, 19, 25-26, 29-30, 32, 34-35, 53, 55, 62-65, 67
Legrain 35, 68, 73, 76-81
Lepsius 65-66
Loret 38, 56, 73-76
MacDonald 38, 72-73
Mariette
- A. 12, 20, 51, 54-55
- S. 15
Maspero 12-17, 19, 26, 29, 31-34, 38, 42, 49-50, 53-55, 61-67, 76-77, 79-80
Melek, Sultana 18
Mohammed Ahmed, Mahdi 15
Mohammed Mohassib 53, 57-58, 80
Morgan, de 35-37, 39, 47, 51, 53, 56, 69-73, 76-78, 80
Müller 81
Murch 78-79
Murray 82
Napoleon 7, 12, 54
Naville 76
Newberry 49, 75
Northampton, Lord 76
Petrie 31, 82
Pleyte
- C.M. 77
- P. 76
- W. 7-8, 14, 17, 20, 23, 25, 29, 34-39, 42-43, 47, 51, 55-56, 58, 61-62, 65-81

Quibell 76
Rainer, Erzherzog 62
Reckers 64
Reclus 13
Reisner 54
Reuvens 7-8
Revillout 35-36, 83
Ricci, de 83
Rochemonteix 16
Sayce 19, 22, 58, 73, 75, 77-79, 82-83
Schelling
- A.J. 14, 23, 25-26, 47, 49, 61
- P. 26, 30
Schiaparelli 54, 80-81
Schweinfurth 55, 66, 79
Serrurier 14, 23, 26
Somers Clark 74, 76
Speelman 70
Spiegelberg 75, 83
Steindorff 29
Stolk, van 18, 80
Stuers, de 31
Templeman van der Hoeven 70
Tewfik, Khedive 12, 14, 17, 20
Toda y Güell 16
Urabi 14
Wiedemann 75
Wijngaarden, van 47
Wilbour 15-19, 32-33, 44, 50, 53, 58, 77
Wilhelmina, Queen 75
William I, King 7
William II, King 7
William III, King 75
Wilson 58, 74
Witkowski 76

2. Persons, ancient

Ahmose 80
Amenhotep II 74
Beshau 24
Diocletian 47
Diptah 30-31
Fetekta 66
Galerius 47

Hatshepsut 76
Heka-ankhu 30-31
Henttawy 55
Henuy 71
Herunefer 24
Hor 31
Istemkheb 37-38, 55, 75
Kheops 65
Maatkare 55
Masaherta 37
Menes 74
Neferrenpet 80
Nesikhonsu 37, 47, 55
Nesitanebashru 36-37, 47
Parthenios 42
Pinodjem I 55
Pinodjem II 37
Probus 47
Psamtekmen 44
Ramesses II 17
Sebekhotep 24
Sennedjem 16, 51
Sesostris 67, 80
Seti I 80
Tjetji 21
Tutankhamun 21

3. Places
Abu Roash 54
Abu Simbel 13
Abusir 66
Abydos 16, 26, 61, 66, 74
Akhmim 16, 23, 25, 29, 31-37, 44, 49-51, 54, 56, 62-65, 67-68
Alexandria 12, 14, 17-18, 20, 69, 71, 83
Amarna 18, 35
Amsterdam 11, 30, 71-73
Armant 34, 38-39, 67, 71, 73, 75, 77-78
Arsinoe 62
Ashmunein 73
Assiut 14-15, 18, 29, 63
Aswan 12, 14-16, 18, 20, 25, 44, 63, 65, 72, 74, 77
Awlad el-Sheikh 23, 25-26
Baarn 11, 29, 32
el-Balyana 15, 26, 29, 62
Beni Suef 18
Bennekom 37, 43-44, 47, 70-71, 75
Biga 63
Bückeburg 11

Bulaq 12, 16-17, 19, 26, 29, 35, 38, 55, 61-64, 66
Cairo 12-23, 26, 30, 32, 38-39, 42, 49-55, 57-58, 62, 64-67, 70, 72-79, 81, 83
Carthage 8, 21
Dahshur 35
Damietta 15
el-Debba 14
Diospolis Magna 33
Dongola 14-15, 72
Elephantine 33, 75
Esna 71
Fayum 62
Gebelein 38-39, 43-44, 51, 56, 67, 71-72, 75, 77-78, 82
Girga 23, 25, 44, 47, 61
Giza 35, 42, 47, 51, 68, 72, 78
the Hague 13, 21, 53, 57-58, 64, 69-70
el-Hawawish 31
el-Hiba 75
Ismailiya 12
Jebel Garra 25
el-Kab 16, 25-26, 61, 74, 76
Karnak 16, 23, 25, 32-33, 37-39, 65, 71, 73-81
Koptos 33, 44
Kurkur 14, 23, 44
Lage Vuursche 22, 62, 64
- Pijnenburg 11, 19, 21-22, 29, 47, 62, 64
Luxor 16-23, 35, 38, 42-43, 47, 52-53, 55-58, 63-65, 67-83
- Palmenburg 19, 21, 43, 53, 56, 58
Maharaqqa 14
Mari Girgis 23, 25
Memphis 26
Menshiya 23
Minia 18
Mo'alla 67
Nag' el-Mashayikh 44, 47
Nile Delta 12, 15
Nubia 12-15, 20, 54, 58
Omdurman 72
Ouderkerk aan den IJssel 26
Philae 63, 74
Port Said 38, 51, 72
Qena 39
Quft 23, 25
Rosetta 17
el-Salmīya 38, 75
Saqqara 15, 18, 55

Semna 14
Sohag 29, 62
Sudan 12, 15, 20-21, 26, 58, 63, 72
Suez Canal 12
Thebes 26, 37, 44, 61-62, 71, 76
- Deir el-Bahari 17, 32, 34, 37, 47, 55, 63-64, 70-71, 76-77
- Deir el-Medineh 16
- Sheikh Abd-el-Qurna 37, 38, 51
- Medinet Habu 39, 70-71, 76-78
- Ramesseum 76
- Valley of the Kings 22, 56
Tod 16, 34, 38
el-Urdi 14
Wadi Halfa 12-15, 26

4. Institutions
Amsterdam University Library 8, 26
Antiquities Service 12-13, 15, 19-21, 32-33, 35, 38, 42, 50-54, 57-58, 76, 79
Austrian National Library 62
Berlin Museum 55, 65, 71
Bibliothèque Nationale 29, 49, 54, 63
Boston Museum of Fine Arts 54
British Museum 21, 49, 55, 63, 78
Brussels Museum 21
Cairo Museum 12, 16-17, 19, 26, 29, 32, 34-35, 38, 42, 44, 49, 51-53, 55, 61-63, 66, 68, 72-73, 76-79, 81
Collège de France 83
Consulate, Alexandria 13, 21, 71
Consulate, Cairo 15, 21, 36, 38-39, 42, 50-51, 53-54, 57-58, 63-64, 67, 69, 71-75, 77-79
Deutsche Orient Gesellschaft 54
Egypt Exploration Fund 54
Geographical Society 8, 15, 26, 65
Harvard University 54
Institut français d'Archéologie orientale 16, 19-20, 32, 54, 66-67, 76
Louvre 35, 54-55, 83
Metropolitan Museum of Art 55
Ministry of Education/Interior 30-31, 50-51, 53-55, 63
Ministry of Foreign Affairs 21, 36, 53-54, 64, 68, 70, 72, 74, 77-78

National Archives, The Hague 13, 21, 53, 57-58
National Coin Collection 47, 75
National Museum of Ethnology 7-8, 14, 23, 26, 49, 64-65, 78
Turin Museum 80, 82
Wilbour Library 19

5. General

amulet 39, 64
antiquities laws 42, 50-54, 58
archive 8, 13-14, 17, 20-21, 34-35, 37, 44, 49, 58, 61-83
bead 78
Book of the Dead 80
brick 37-39, 50, 59, 75
canopic jar 44
cartonnage 30, 59, 64
cemetery 22, 26, 31, 33-34, 38-39, 50-51, 56, 82
coffin 30-31, 44, 49, 59, 64
coin 42, 47, 55-56, 59, 74-77, 79
Coptic manuscript 26-29, 35, 49-50, 54, 56, 59, 62-63, 75, 80
customs 51-52, 62, 74, 77
dahabiya 12, 14-16, 18, 57-58
dealer 9, 19, 21, 23, 26, 29, 32-33, 36, 39, 43, 49-54, 58, 63-64, 67, 70, 72, 78-81
dealer's license 52
diplomatic courier 36, 50, 69
donation 14, 23, 25-26, 33, 43-44, 47, 49, 58
door jamb 67
duplicate 32, 34, 55, 63, 66
ethnography 23, 26, 44, 59
excavation permit 13, 51
excavations 7, 29, 31-34, 38, 44, 47, 50-56, 62, 75-76, 82
export permit 26, 29, 36, 42, 50-54, 57, 62, 69
figurine 39-40, 42, 59, 77-78
flint implement 23, 25, 38-40, 59, 77, 79-81
forgeries 17, 37-39, 42, 46-47, 59, 73, 75-77, 80-81
funerary cone 43-44
heritage 51, 54, 58
immunity 52-53, 57
ivory 39, 80
jewellery 55

mace-head 39, 41
monastery 25, 29, 31, 33, 50, 62
mummy 17, 26, 29-32, 34-37, 44-47, 49-50, 59, 61-64, 71, 82
offering table 39, 41, 44, 55, 77
ostracon 23, 25, 32-33, 35, 37-39, 49-51, 55-56, 59, 65, 67, 69, 71-75, 77-78, 81
palette 38-39, 41
papyrus 35, 42, 46-47, 50, 56, 67-68, 72, 76, 78, 80-81, 83
Papyrus Insinger 8, 20, 32, 35-36, 43, 50, 55-57, 59, 67-70, 79, 81, 83
partage 51, 54, 62-63
photography 8, 11, 13-20, 23, 34-35, 44, 61, 64-67, 79
plunder 29, 31, 33, 35, 54, 79, 82
politics 11-12, 14, 20, 54
Ptah-Sokar-Osiris figure 43-44
publication 7, 29, 36, 62, 65-67, 72, 75-77, 79-80, 82
relief 55
revolt 14-15, 20, 72
royal cache 17-18, 32, 34, 37, 47, 50, 55, 77
seal 43-44, 46-47, 78-79, 82
sebakh 33, 37, 50, 52, 71
shabti 32, 39, 44, 55, 63-64, 77
statue 32, 44, 55, 64, 76
steamer 14-16, 18, 22, 72-73
stela 21-22, 24-26, 32, 42, 50, 55, 59, 61, 64, 72, 76, 80
temple 13-14, 16, 25-26, 33-34, 39, 47, 50, 52, 70-73, 75-76
terracotta 39-42, 44, 55, 78
textile 17, 26, 32-37, 47, 50, 54, 56, 59, 61-62, 64-65, 71, 77-78
tomb 16-18, 22, 26, 31, 37, 54, 61, 67, 71, 74, 77, 80
transport costs 29, 49-50, 58, 65, 68-69, 73, 76-77
travel account 8, 13-14, 21
tuberculosis 11-12, 22
unwrapping 17, 37, 64, 71
vessel
- glass 39-40, 55, 59
- pottery 14, 23-25, 32-33, 35, 38-41, 44-47, 50-51, 55-56, 59, 76-82
- stone 25-26, 59, 61
visitation 36, 42, 51-52, 69